John Tunis, Henry C. Potter

The Faith by which we stand

Sermons

John Tunis, Henry C. Potter

The Faith by which we stand
Sermons

ISBN/EAN: 9783743350236

Manufactured in Europe, USA, Canada, Australia, Japa

Cover: Foto ©Lupo / pixelio.de

Manufactured and distributed by brebook publishing software (www.brebook.com)

John Tunis, Henry C. Potter

The Faith by which we stand

THE FAITH BY WHICH WE STAND

THE
FAITH BY WHICH WE STAND

Sermons

BY

THE REV. JOHN TUNIS
LATE RECTOR OF GRACE CHURCH, MILBROOK, N. Y.

WITH INTRODUCTION BY
THE RT. REV. HENRY C. POTTER, D.D.
BISHOP OF NEW YORK.

NEW YORK
JAMES POTT & COMPANY
FOURTH AVENUE & 22D ST.
1896

IN
LOVING REMEMBRANCE
OF
ONE WHO WALKED WITH GOD
"HE WAS NOT; FOR GOD TOOK HIM"

INTRODUCTION

THE Rev. John Tunis was born in the city of New York, December 23, 1858, and died at the rectory of Grace Church, Millbrook, N. Y., August 18, 1896, being, therefore, at the time of his death but thirty-seven years of age.

He entered the College of the City of New York in 1873, and left it, on account of ill health, without graduating. In June, 1882, he graduated at the Harvard Divinity School, and later entered the Unitarian ministry, becoming an instructor in the Meadville Theological Seminary, and later pastor of a Unitarian congregation at Quincy, Ill. Subsequently he entered the senior class of Harvard University, and received the degree of A.B. in 1891.

Having undergone a radical change in his theological and ecclesiastical convictions, he became a candidate for holy orders in the diocese of New York, and was ordained to the diaconate in February, 1893, and to the priesthood in the following year. He was, during his diaconate and until

INTRODUCTION

November, 1895, minister in charge of the Church of the Epiphany, New York City, when he became rector of Grace Church, Millbrook.

No hand but his own could fully write the intellectual and spiritual history of his brief but not uneventful life. He had a profound and controlling love of the truth and sought it earnestly and reverently. Deprived of wise and sympathetic guidance at a critical period in his student life, he followed the leading of his earlier convictions out of and away from his earlier fellowships, only to find, with wider reading and larger reflection, that the household of faith in which he had been born was the only one which offered to him the satisfaction of his intellectual convictions and of his highest spiritual aspirations.

How strong were the former and how lofty and clear-visioned the latter, the sermons that follow will show. They are not the sermons of a controversialist, but of a true prophet and messenger of the Eternal, touching and enriching the most familiar themes with the fine insight of a singularly pure and direct spiritual faculty. No one ever heard Mr. Tunis preach without the conviction that he was listening to a true seer—one with the vision to discern, and with the gift to translate that which he saw. His sermons have the rare charm of a clear, direct, and scholarly style, a delightful naturalness which makes them models for all preachers, and, best of all, they illumine that of which they speak. The sermon in this volume entitled "The Privilege of Power" is a signal illustration of these qualities. It takes an incident in the earthly ministry of Christ, and from the first word to the last lifts it to the height of its greater meaning with a sureness of touch, felicity of illustration, and a firm grasp of its highest spiritual message which are irresistible.

To have lost so prematurely, as it seems to us, such a voice, out of a generation that so sorely needs voices that have in them a lifting quality, is verily to be greatly bereaved. It will be some compensation to those who knew and loved him to have these sermons, the spell of which, as they listened to them, they will never forget. And there are others, I venture to think, who will be glad to learn from these pages that God is still speaking by the mouth of His holy prophets, and to find in them a new inspiration to hold fast to the things that have been most clearly revealed and "are most surely believed among us."

HENRY C. POTTER.

NEW YORK, Advent, 1896.

CONTENTS

	PAGE
PEACE	9
THE INCARNATION	21
"AND HE SAID, COME"	33
"FOLLOW ME"	45
JESUS ONLY	57
THE PRIVILEGE OF POWER	69
THE JOURNEY TO JERUSALEM	79
PRAYER	91
LENT	105
GOOD FRIDAY	117
EASTER	129
THE SECRET OF COURAGE	141
WHITSUNDAY	153
ASCENSION-DAY	167
MIRACLES	179
TRINITY-SUNDAY	191
A FIXED HEART	205
THE HOLY COMMUNION	217

PEACE

Ps. xxxvii. 37.

The end of that man is peace.

PEACE

THERE was something in the very situation of their country that made the idea of peace especially dear to the Jews. For centuries Palestine was the natural battle-ground for the contending armies of the world. Palestine in those days was what Italy was in the middle ages, or Belgium in more recent times: the fighting-ground for the surrounding nations. The armies of Assyria and Egypt met within sight of the Holy City. The great highways of trade passed through Palestine, and the quiet of Judea was interrupted by the commerce and the ambition of the great kings of the East. When we remember that almost every great soldier of the Old World came within sight of Jerusalem we understand better that longing desire and craving for peace which the Jews felt. The Pharaohs of Egypt fought out their campaigns in Judea. Nebuchadnezzar went there from Babylon, Alexander the Great from Greece, Pompey and Titus from Rome. What was merely an incident in the annals of Egypt or Assyria or Babylon was one of a succession of death-struggles to Judea. Out of its own deep experience, then, the nation speaks through the words of the psalmist: "My soul hath long dwelt among them that are enemies unto peace. I labor for peace; but when I speak unto them thereof, they make them ready to battle."

Nothing in all the Bible is more interesting than just the chain of passages in which the word "peace" is used; and no one can read that succession of cries and pleadings, imprecations and blessings, without being struck at the wonderful development which the idea of peace itself underwent at the hands of the Jews. It began as the simple and strong prayer to be let alone. But in the throes of war the heart of the nation deepened and expanded till it dawned on the Jews that there was something a vast deal truer and sweeter than the mere immunity from invasion or internal disturbance. They began to see that in all the battle and confusion there was a moral law vindicated, and that there could not be any peace until iniquity was judged. The prophet Jeremiah, that fine spirit fallen on the evil days of the dying nation, scorned the very proposals of peace, because at that time any peace or truce was in his eyes but the vain postponement of the inevitable retribution of the Lord.

When our Lord speaks of peace it is very plain

that He speaks of no mere tranquillity or freedom from conflict. One feels instinctively in His words something that has been hard-earned. There is the sound of something fought for and conquered. "My peace I leave with you, My peace I give unto you: not as the world giveth, give I unto you. . . . In the world ye shall have tribulation: but be of good cheer; I have overcome the world."

And then St. Paul says the fruit of the Spirit is peace. It is not the first flower and evidence of the life of Christ in us, but it is the fruit: it comes last of all. A man's first experiences in trying to be a Christian are often anything but peace. The Christian's deep and untroubled peace comes after labor and long patience, after many storms and winds, after many scorching days. Its serene glow is the fruit of all the burden and heat of the day. "The *end* of that man is peace."

The Bible looks on man's life here as a battle, or at the least as a school and time of searching. That is the dramatic way the Bible treats of human life. There is a beginning and a middle and an end to it. The Bible teaches us that life begins as a trust, and continues as a struggle, and it ends as peace. There is always something at stake and there is always a crown for him who triumphs.

A man is set here in the world in the midst of

a vast struggle; he is born into it, and the only door out of it is his death. No one can hope to escape his life's battle; the one thing each man can hope to do is to see the hand of his Captain flashing here and there as the hosts of righteousness are charged into the battle. How can a man dream of drawing back into his own seclusion and safety when the world battle is on? How dare he stand back from the swelling ranks of the soldiers of the redemption? No man can live unto himself alone in this world; no man can be a mere onlooker. He is either swept along in the current of salvation or swept out with the shattered columns of those who withstood their Lord. It is not possible to stand still, to settle down with one's gain or with one's loss, with one's joy or with one's grief, with one's peace now or with one's discontent now. One must take sides; one must hear the cry, "Who is on the Lord's side?" The real key to all this world's pride and glory is the silent rush of divine Providence to the eternal rescue of man. There is nothing but power and opportunity intrusted here, nothing but toil and dust and confusion; but at the end, peace.

If you seek the peace of your life at the outset and independent of exertion or anxiety or sacrifice, if you try to get peace by avoiding hard things, hard places, or unpleasant tasks, you will surely miss it. The end of that man is infinite weariness and chagrin. Peace is the feeling at the last that a man has been faithful from the beginning. The kind of confidence which a man brings out of his life's battle depends on the kind of character which he put into that life's battle. That is the reason why the end of that brave, patient, overburdened, dauntless man is peace; his character has been shown in everything he undertook, and his peace comes in the joy that he has used well his noblest powers. Such a man expects toil and backset and hard lines and uncomfortable situations; he does not expect his peace at first; he would suspect it of being a lure and a cheat if it were offered him then. "The end of that man is peace," he says to himself continually. That is the hymn that sings itself into all the hours of his labor and watching and self-denial; he counts on the present being a time of tension and tumult and struggle. There is always before his eye the dream of an end; he seems to see through the smoke of this present time and hear through the din of the passing days a vision and a voice. The one is the hand that holds out to him all he counts dear, and the other is the word of praise that confers the crown. Then he goes back to his life's conflict and deals harder blows than ever for that end. If it were pleasant now, if there were nothing hard now, if he had peace in his heart now, then there would be no peace at the end. Oh, it is long now, and weary waiting, and our arms ache with their loads, and our very hearts seem tired and droop. It seems as though all we could do was to try to keep step with Christ, until on a day there comes a pause, and we look up: the goal is reached, and at the end, peace.

I hear a man say that there can be no God, because if there was an all-wise and all-powerful God, He would have made the world perfect at once and would have granted human happiness outright and complete. That is the most common practical objection of skepticism. But the Christian who has once seized the dramatic note of all Christian history has only to answer in the words of the text, "The *end* of that man is peace." Doubtless God could have made the world at a stroke and man happy by one gift of divine grace, but that would have been a dead world and a soulless man; it would not have been you and I, who are made the stronger for our burdens, the wiser for our mistakes, and the holier for our sorrows. We should have grown weary to death of such a mechanical world. This world was ordained by God to be the task through which we should inherit the promises. God could have given us peace at the beginning, instead of leaving it to be the dream and the vision of all human effort and loyalty, but it would have been the death of the soul. When God planned, my brother, to make us in our possibilities little lower than the angels, He whispered to the shining company about His throne, "The end of that man is peace." He put peace there at the end, when all was tried and fought and won; for if He had given it to us at the first we should have ceased to aspire to better things, and with aspiring we should have ceased to be men.

By and by there comes a day when we realize that our peace and happiness are to come after our efforts and because of our efforts, and that there is no kind of peace or happiness which can satisfy a human soul except it comes in and through its own sense of having done its duty, and then half the problems of our lives and all the complainings are set at rest. Peace without the strain, without slipping, without sorrow, without enemies, peace merely through settling back and withdrawal, there is nothing in all this for a Christian; he is not the man whom the writer of the psalm singled out as the perfect man and upright. You see him sometimes. He is perhaps only an ordinary man forcing himself to do extraordinary things under the weight of his responsibilities. He bears immense burdens; he fights at great odds; he has secret sorrows; he has to do disagreeable things; he finds himself in very unpleasant situations; he has to crush his own inclinations, but he has gotten firmly in mind the idea that the end only of a man's life can be peace, and so he strives with a strength greater than his own. Nothing stops him, nothing demeans him, there is nothing too laborious or too exacting; but he knows that not one pain or labor shall be forgotten by his Father.

Peace at the last! It is the fruit of all the faithfulness, all the perseverance, all the courage, all the carefulness, all the faith of a man's life. Then comes the end, when toil is rewarded, pain is transfigured, doubt is illuminated, steadfastness is glorified. And how sweet that end is to the man who has kept true, who in spite of his mistakes and his wanderings and his discouragements and his sins has kept his eye on his Lord! That is peace, a deep joy that reverberates through a man's whole being. One moment of that peace is sweeter than a lifetime of the world. If it were only a moment in which a man could stand in heaven and feel that all was done, the faith kept, and the battle won, it would be worth all the struggle here on earth. One moment of peace, with

> " Sorrow vanquished, labor ended,
> Jordan past,"

would more than outweigh all that a man had undergone to reach it. Christ treasures up

PEACE

everything we have done to reach His peace. Surely, if He said that not a sparrow falls to the ground without our heavenly Father, then also without Him there falls to the ground not one bruised heart, not one broken will, not one weight of care or pang of grief, not one cry or prayer or effort or watch well kept; but they are all numbered and remembered in that peace which this world can neither give nor take away.

THE INCARNATION

St. Luke II. 28–30.

Then took he Him up in his arms, and blessed God, and said, Lord, now lettest Thou Thy servant depart in peace, according to Thy word: for mine eyes have seen Thy salvation.

THE INCARNATION

THERE was a man in Jerusalem whose name was Simeon, and who was a just and a devout Jew, filled with the expectation of his people that at length they should be redeemed from all their sorrows by the Messiah who should be born among them. Simeon must have been a man well advanced in years; he had come to that mellow time in a good man's life when it is enough to make him happy to watch the younger life about him. There were no more prizes for him to gain; he could not run any longer in the hot race of life. Whatever he had gained or learned or enjoyed, that he must be satisfied with; and whatever he wanted to do or acquire or win, that he must leave for others. He saw young people about him, who had the strength that had left him, and who had the power to grasp the new ideas that he could not entertain; but he did not settle back into a querulous and discontented old age; he filled himself with the kindliness and the generosity and the friendliness of an old man who was glad to cheer others on to the prizes that he could not hope to get himself. The man who is no longer able to bear his part in the rivalries and competition of young men, and who tries no longer to keep abreast with the runners, to be the first in trade, or at the top of his profession, or to be known for his success, but who simply waits on till God calls him, and in the meanwhile spends his last treasure of strength in cheering the others, in doing kindly services, in words of hope and encouragement, that holiness of the aged Simeons, who are in every age and in every community, does more to make life seem sweet and to shame sin out of men's hearts than all the lessons of all the books that ever were written.

So Simeon, the just and devout old man in Jerusalem, went daily into the temple. He was full of the great dream that swam in the eye of every devout Jew, that Messiah was to be born to redeem His people. It had been revealed to him that he should not see death before he had seen the Lord's Christ.

One day, as he came into the temple for his usual devotions, there happened to him all that he had waited and prayed for; for as a little child was brought into the temple to be presented to the Lord, as the custom was, the old man knew that it had at last come and the hour of his country's deliverance was at hand. "Then took he Him up in his arms, and blessed God, and said, Lord, now lettest Thou Thy servant depart in peace, according to Thy word: for mine eyes have seen Thy salvation, which Thou hast prepared before the face of all people; a light to lighten the Gentiles, and the glory of Thy people Israel."

That moment in Simeon's life, when he felt in his arms the Lord's Christ and knew that the dream of his nation for centuries was at last fulfilled, must have been worth to him all the years of his patient waiting, all the hours of resignation, all the pain of giving up his own life and standing aside to let others go ahead. The right to hold the infant Christ in his arms must have come as the reward of all his prayers and his devotions and his piety. He must have had friends and companions who spent their age in dwelling on their infirmities or in despondent comments on the time they had lived to see, and who looked with little favor on Simeon's instinct for piety; but it was given to an old man's resignation and an old man's holiness to take up in his arms the Lord's Christ. Then he, who had simply watched and waited in his faith and prayers, broke out into the strain of prophecy that the church will forever use to hail the Lord. That was a rich reward for a life of prayer.

The child that Simeon held in his arms was the incarnate Son of God. We believe that almighty God, our heavenly Father, gave His only begotten Son, who laid aside His heavenly nature and left His heavenly home and took upon Him the nature of man and was born of a pure virgin. One's mind fails one in trying to think of all that is meant by the Incarnation, and words seem to contain the truth no more than a flask will contain the sunshine. If there were not God forever pouring His truth through our words, whether we think of it or no, the very words that are the best we could do to describe it would seem like a mockery. Look at the world that is about you; remember all that is in it, all the races of living men and women who inhabit it; look up at night and see the stars, which we know are vastly larger than our earth, and for all we know are inhabited by thinking beings like ourselves. Now He who made all these, who knows what is going on in every planet, and who guides what is going on, was able to humble Himself and to limit and confine His being, and to come to earth and be born as a little child; and that just and devout man, who hung about the temple waiting for the consolation of Israel, lifted Him up in his arms and said, "Lord, now lettest Thou Thy servant depart in peace, according to Thy word: for mine eyes have seen Thy salvation."

Do not mind, brethren, if this thought is inconceivable to you; do not mind if your heart is full of perplexing doubts when you say these words in the creed: "And was made man." It is very hard to believe; it is so hard to believe that, except God stood back of the words and the thoughts which we say and think, and pushed our faith, there is hardly one of us who could believe. We believe it not because we can understand, but because God has made our hearts so that we cannot help believing if we are in a devout frame of mind. Whenever man lets go this faith something truer than man's own thoughts forces him back to faith again. An old Christian writer sums up this miracle of the Incarnation in a way that brings home to us its awful mystery: "He who should lie in the Father's bosom was born of a virgin, and He who went on the wings of the wind lay in a mother's arms, and He who was worshiped by the angels of heaven was supping with the publicans on earth, and He whom the seraphim dared not gaze at was questioned by Pilate and condemned to death."

The incarnation of the divine Son means that our Lord took human nature and was made man. He did not become *a man*, He did not take the nature of *a man*, so that He became a man among men; He took on Him human nature and, as our creed says, "He was made man." He was one person and remains one person. His human nature and His divine nature are equally real; neither one extinguishes the other. He is very man and very God. This manhood is always real and our Lord was really born. He really grew and His body strengthened and His mind enlarged. Our Lord did not pretend to be born or merely play at being a child. He was really tempted and He really suffered and really died. On the other hand, He was really God. He was born by the power of the Holy Ghost; and when He went into the temple with His parents He knew He must be about His Father's business; and when He was tempted He really had power to "command that these stones be made bread." He did really feed the five thousand, and raised Lazarus from the dead, and He did really and truly rise again after three days and ascended into heaven. The truth of the Incarnation is in the real and eternal union of the human and the divine natures in the one person of our blessed Lord.

It was man's nature, and not the nature of any one man, that our Lord took upon Him. The divine Son did not choose out one life among all human lives and incarnate Himself in that one life. That would separate Christ from all the rest of mankind. Our Lord was not one individual merely of the human race, born in the natural order, and then miraculously united to God in the person of the Son. That might glorify one particular man, but the truth of the Incarnation is that all human nature was glorified. This is the greatest miracle of all: our Lord Jesus Christ is the power of God united to all human nature—not to one individual human nature, but all human nature. He came and redeemed *man*, not a few men. He glorified not a few people, but the race. He has entered into the nature not of one man, but of all men everywhere and for all time. He took on Him the nature of man in the days of the Pharisees, and He has taken on Him the nature of us men born in these last days. It removes a good deal of the difficulty to admit that it is impossible for almighty God to narrow His life down to that of a single individual human being. That is inconceivable and that is untrue. But our Lord in being born of the Virgin Mary took to Him all human nature, all human nature of all time and of all men everywhere, and that truth is not only not impossible, but it is divinely true. If there are human beings in other worlds than ours, then that human nature too must be taken by our Lord. He who came to seek and to save that which was lost could not leave human nature anywhere defenseless, anywhere unredeemed. He came to cast out all the sins, to soothe all the sorrows, and to raise up all the dead wherever it might be.

When Simeon held that infant Christ in his arms he felt in some dim way this miracle of the Incarnation. He could not have felt so if it were simply one life that was glorified by being taken up and united by the divine Son. That devout old man was charged with the spirit of prophecy because he dimly appreciated the truth that all human nature everywhere was being drawn to Christ and being redeemed. Something stirs in your heart; that is Christ moving in your soul. Something moves you to pity, moves you to be willing to wait, moves you to forgive and to repent and to pray and adore; that is Christ moving in your soul. Christ is the moral center of the universe and is the deep heart of all human nature. All things turn about Him, and all the struggles of man seem grand when we know whose power is working in man. In all the history of man on the earth, in all the toil and pain and battle and wanderings, human eyes see only confusion; but Christ sees a new and divine order slowly working out into peace. Oh, through what a mystery of training He leads us until, through our suffering and our trials, that divine nature to which ours is eternally joined is able to reveal itself! There it is; all the time there it is, the mystery of the Incarnation in our human nature. Through our tears and our doubts and our cries and our prayers Christ is starting forth in our lives. Comforts that we never dreamed of, and strength we never suspected, and peace that seemed impossible, all these things slowly work through the hard, tough material of our sinful human nature. It does not come all at once. Christ is not born for us suddenly in all the power of His divine person; but as we pray and wait like that devout Simeon, and live daily in the temple, and bring ourselves little by little to think everything of being like Christ, and less and less of being like the world, then He is revealed to us. Our Lord will be born to us after we have watched long enough, and borne patiently enough, and prayed fervently enough; our Lord will be born to us too as a little child, and we too shall hold Him in our arms.

Brethren, remember the lesson of Simeon. There are those who in some mysterious providence of God are no longer able to do their share of this world's labor. They can, like Simeon, however, more than make up for that loss by their kindliness and devoutness. They may for one reason or another have become worth little to the world for what they can do with their hands; but how much more they can be worth to the world for their prayers! They may be no longer a power by their efforts, but they can be a far greater power to all men about them by their piety. God has mysteriously ordered it so that the influence which one cannot acquire through activity and bodily strength can be accomplished through our holiness. Nothing that Simeon ever accomplished through the work of his hands equaled the good that he did through the holiness of his heart.

"AND HE SAID, COME"

St. Matt. xiv. 28.

And Peter answered Him and said, Lord, if it be Thou, bid me come unto Thee on the water.

"AND HE SAID, COME"

JESUS had fed the multitude and then sent the disciples away in a boat, while He Himself went up into a mountain apart to pray; and when the evening was come He was there alone. By that time the disciples were far out on the lake, toiling heavily at the oars; for the wind was contrary and the sea tossed with waves. Suddenly He whom they had left behind was seen walking on the water. The disciples cried out for fear, because it seemed to them like the sign of some impending disaster; but our Lord with a quiet word of reassurance said, "It is I; be not afraid." At that Peter, always the soldier spirit of the apostles, answered Him, "Lord, if it be Thou, bid me come unto Thee on the water." How swift and clear was the answer: "And He said, Come"!

Our Lord accepted at once the test that Peter set: "Lord, if it *be* Thou, bid me come unto Thee on the water." That was a marvelous insight of Peter. To the eyes of the disciples, strained with the anxious watch of the sea, suddenly the Lord appeared. It sent a deadly chill into their hearts. Peter, however, felt instantly that if it were indeed the Lord walking on the water, then he could go to Him. It was, you see, the practical man who immediately put the vision to the test of reality; but you see also that, while the other disciples were paralyzed with fear and superstition, it was this practical man who alone grasped the vision. Peter's nature was at the same time extremely practical and highly visionary. The great leaders of men have a mind that is, on the one hand, concrete and practical, and, on the other hand, soaring and believing and visionary; they are full of affairs and details, and then they are also full of insight and penetration. St. Peter was the man of business among the apostles, but then there are more visions recorded of him than of any other of the Twelve. That was Peter, the soldier apostle and the man of dreams; the man who always put everything at once to the test of reality, but the man also who was quicker than all the others to acknowledge the Lord. While the rest of the frightened apostles were struggling with their superstitions, this man of vision and of power was clambering down the side of the ship to go to Jesus.

It is wonderful to study the influence of our Lord on Peter's character. It seemed as though in contact with Jesus every characteristic strength and every characteristic weakness started up and stood out in bold relief. Peter's practical nature was marvelously satisfied by our Lord; something about the person of the Lord seemed to steady and fortify the whole man in Peter. His spirit must have fed on our Lord's spirit as really as a man eats bread and meat. Jesus was so full of truth, and yet so full of reality, Peter felt the joy of finding a life that was as real and human as he was, but which combined with it a vision of truth and holiness beyond anything Peter ever knew before.

So when Peter saw the vision of the Lord walking on the water he saw One who always strengthened his soul and purified his whole heart. If that is Christ, then that is the Lord in whose presence everything is possible to me; if that is Christ, then that is the Lord who fills my soul with courage and with peace. Peter knew that he had only to go to Christ on the water to become at every step bolder, stronger, and surer. It is the passion of a man's whole soul that cries, "Lord, if it be Thou, bid me come unto Thee on the water." And then he heard with such a sense of joy the old and satisfying sound of his Master's voice, calm and certain and assuring, "Come." "And He said, Come."

Jesus has answered many a soldier heart since

then in the same way. Often have His servants cried out to Him to know whether in this storm-beaten world the Lord was really there, and how quickly He has answered back! He has always met Peter's test. He answered Pilate nothing, for He would not endure Pilate's test. But Thomas, who was sincere, though he was slow of faith, he suffered to put his hands into the very print of the nails. He will spurn no honest cry to Him to show Himself the Lord. Men have looked up from the struggles of this world disheartened, sinking, almost ready to give up, and they have cried out to what seemed like a vision of Christ on the sea that was overwhelming His servants, "Lord, if it be Thou, bid me come unto Thee on the water." "And He said, Come." Time after time the Lord has answered back the men who felt themselves going down under this world's injustice and tyranny, "And He said, Come." What a sound that must have been to Athanasius in the fourth century, when he seemed to stand alone before the storm of human rancor and malice! He heard only his Lord saying across the waters, "Come." What must have been that command to come when, in the fifth century, Christian Europe lay prostrate before the armies of the heathen heroes! Suddenly men looked at the cross, and the blessed word seemed fairly to speak over the sea of their desolation, "And He said, Come." We think of our own times, brethren, as wonderful, because knowledge and culture and the arts have done so much to refine and lighten our cares. Never forget, however, that those were the times of heroism and Christian daring; those were the times when this world was all dark and Calvary was a cross of fire shining out of the darkness. The privilege of living is not all on our side to-day. There are many things to-day to make life comfortable, but there have been times when there were more things to make living sublime. There have been times when the air was charged with inspiration. The world was crude and simple and unlearned, and in parts barbarous, and life was hard and stormy with waves; but across the boisterous waters there was Christ walking on the sea, and men cried to Him in their despair to save country and church, and even civilization, "And He said, Come."

We must all in some way or other have gone through this experience of testing Christ. We come to a point sometimes where we ask how God can exist and the world be what it is; that is testing Christ. It could have seemed no harder to Peter to walk on the water to Christ than it seems to us at times to serve Him and be true to Him in the midst of a contrary world. It is very hard in this world to walk erect and spotless and uncontaminated. The vision of Christ and Christ's church must seem to many men an impossible vision. God puts some of our fellow-men in places that are so burdened and thwarted that it must be very hard to keep on believing in a just and good God. These men have to fight to keep alive the faith that you and I give scarcely a thought to, but how Christ must prize the fidelity of such men who keep firm in spite of all! Do you suppose that we are here, and the rough, churchless, Christless, friendless men are all there, in the mine, in the furnace-room, in the barracks, on the patrol, and that we are believers solely by our power of faith, and that they are unbelievers solely by their want of faith? No; if some of us were where they are, and they were in our places, would not they be to-day praising God, and should not we be there denying Him? Christ knows the truth about that, and where toil is very heavy, and where sin is almost a custom, and men cry out of their despair, with what a full, strong, jubilant voice He must say, "Come"! It is always our Lord who is glad to meet the hardest tests. Christ knows that of all His children there is just one thing that every one can do in any place and under any burden, in any loss, in any sorrow, and that is to be brave. "Lord," we say to Him, standing over there in the darkness and across the special trial of our lives, "Lord, if it were really Thou there, I should be able to cross these waters; Lord, if it were really Thou there, I should be able to conquer my failings and to be a better man than my surroundings make me. If it were only Thou there, I could live in the midst of corruption and not become corrupt myself. I could see others take evil advantages and not fall myself under the temptation. I could endure the strain or the cross that is put upon me. I could keep patient under provocation, kind under anxiety, gentle under wrong, true under sorrow, strong in a world where almost all men seem weak. Lord, I could come to Thee if it were only Thou standing there. If it were only Thou, Lord, standing there, I could look death in the face and not falter." "And He said, Come." "And He said, Come."

You cannot bring any test that your Lord has not long ago met and answered. There is no test of pain or privation or hardship or suffering or disappointment or defeat that He has not long ago turned it into His triumph. In the midst of the universal corruption of France in the seventeenth century, Colbert, the king's minister, was incorruptible. There were many worldly priests in his day, but Fénelon was not one of them. When every one about the court was craven, Marie Antoinette was queenly. There have been men uncrushed in misfortune, as Scott; there have been men who made a new ambition for themselves, like Fawcett when he lost the sight of his eyes. It was when the obstacles seemed insuperable that Wolfe dragged himself from the sick-bed and captured Quebec. It does not matter what everybody else is; one need not be like everybody else. One need only hear his Lord say, "Come."

Do not be dismayed; do not be a man forever up and down in his faith, now trustful and now cast down, now eager and now listless, now unable to do enough for your Lord, and now unable to lift a finger for Him. Be for Christ all the time, when He comes and when He goes, when He draws near and when He draws apart. You only need to know that He is on the field, your Captain, and that every soldier has taken from Him the word of command; you only need to know that when He charged you to this war He said, "Lo, I am with you alway, even unto the end of the world." And then you face around to your enemy, and all your soul flows down into your arm, and you are brave with God. Oh, we are hungry here and athirst here for the Christ who wants hard things from us! If Christ only wants my easy struggles, my light burdens, my careless victories, why, I cannot live on such a bread of life; I must have the Christ who expects me to stand firm in a dark time, who looks to me to be bold enough to go and sell all that I have and follow Him. That is the proof that I am not following a dream of my own imagination. My own dream would tell me to be at ease, to risk nothing, to wait until the storm had passed before I took my post. You know that is not Christ; you know it is Christ alone who says out of the very heart of the storm, "Come;" and then straightway something in us, God alone knows what it is, rises within us to walk on the water to go to Jesus. He means we should overcome every difficulty in which we will not let ourselves be tired out, and solve every doubt of which we will take the trouble to think out clearly the terms, and win every battle in which we can still carry peace in the heart. He has a way out of every sorrow in which you will give Him a disciple's trust. "Lord, if it be Thou, bid me come unto Thee on the water. And He said, Come." Then all the man in you, all the soldier in you, all the Christian in you, crowds up to your lips to say, "My Lord," and then, without wondering any longer whether it can be indeed He, we go to Him, who is forever waiting to prove Himself the only Master of a human soul, the only source of peace and power, Christ, the light of the world and the solace of men.

"FOLLOW ME"

St. Matt. ix. 9.

And as Jesus passed forth from thence, He saw a man, named Matthew, sitting at the receipt of custom: and He saith unto him, Follow Me. And he arose, and followed Him.

"FOLLOW ME"

YOU will remember how our Lord called Matthew while he sat at his seat at the customs, and how he left it instantly to become a servant of Christ. It must have come just at the crisis of his life. He reached a point where his whole heart cried out in him for light and guidance, and then his Master called him. It is the marvelous coincidence that we find in the lives of so many of the world's leaders, and which we have in mind when we say of a great hero's success that the hour and the man came together. At the moment when Matthew's own train of thought had brought him to the point of yearning for Christ, at that moment Christ stood before the man and said, " Follow Me. And he arose, and followed Him."

All day long Matthew sat within the shadow of the wall of the city gate and levied the tax on the merchandise that passed along the great highway of trade with Damascus. It is well known that certain trades have disposed men to speculation. The English weavers have furnished many of the radicals of that nation, while poets, philosophers, and mystics of the first rank have come from the shoemaker's bench. It was so with Matthew. The mind of the publican had been working long before Christ came. The ill repute in which his office was held by the strict Jews had made him in self-defense a liberal. He was therefore peculiarly receptive to the new ideas which passed through his mind at the same time as the coins of all nations passed through his hands. His calling made this outcast Jew acquainted with the religious ideas of other nations. The provincialism of the Jew soon gave way as the range of his mind was gradually broadened. He felt the absurdity of the provincial presumption; he felt how empty was the claim of the Jews to alone have the truth, as the march of nations vaster, older, and more learned passed through the Jewish tax-gatherer's gate. Had he been a less serious man, he would have ended by massing all religious beliefs in one common distrust. In the long intervals of quiet, as he sat sheltered from the hot Syrian sun and mused on the tide of peoples passing before him, he dreamed of some comprehensive faith and some all-including deity in which these various worships should be blended into one. Out of all this diversion there should arise union, and out of this diversity there should issue forth a common object of adoration. Perhaps here the man started up at an idea which must have seemed new and wonderful, and then Christ stood before him and said, "Follow Me."

Something in our Lord's manner must have made Matthew feel that here was the solution of all his doubts and here was the end of all his dreams. When Christ the man stood before him and said, "Follow Me," he felt a truth that was higher than anything he could piece together from his varied experiences. No mere abstract immensity such as he could conjure up in cold contemplation could thrill him as the voice of the Master, who came saying, "Follow Me." No matter what may have struck his reason, the Son of man satisfied his heart.

Now the doubt that struggled in Matthew's heart is the same doubt that is struggling in men's hearts to-day. It is not a doubt of all religion, but a doubt whether any one form of historic faith like Christianity can to-day stand apart and claim to be absolute truth. There is no real question to-day that religion in some form is the higher life of man; the doubt that touches men to-day is whether Christianity can continue the claim of being absolute truth. The growth of traffic and intercourse has shown men that there are other religions besides the religion of

Christ. They are as moral and as learned as Christianity. The new intercourse with India and Persia and China and Japan has opened men's eyes, and some of the characteristics of Christianity have been discovered in the religion of Buddha and of Zoroaster. Superficial minds make this discovery a reason for rejecting all religious faith; but the question the devout radical asks of the church is whether the final religion of mankind must not be made up of elements from all the faiths; whether the Bible of the race must not supersede the Scriptures of the Jews; and whether our Lord must not take His place in the general leveling of a religious pantheon.

But as a matter of fact such efforts to establish a religion through an amalgam of all the faiths have been repeatedly made during this century, and have repeatedly failed. The reason is that such universal religion is utterly abstract and is powerless to influence men away from the personal call of Christ. When the robust faith in Christ is weakened down to the mere common denominator of all the creeds, then it is found to be characterless and powerless. That is because nothing is left but an abstraction. So long as it is an abstraction it will be utterly weak. There is an insidious idea abroad among men, and Christians are only too apt to acquiesce in it, that these abstractions of universality and infinity and eternity are more intellectual ideas than that of personality, and that therefore the personal religion of Christ must take second rank to these efforts after a world faith. One cannot say too strongly that this is not so, but that the deepest idea of the human intellect is the idea of personality. These universal creeds do not die because they are more intellectual than the religion of Christ, but because they are less so. These ideas of immensity and vastness of time or space are by no means the strongest ideas of the mind; in fact, they are among the weakest ideas, because they are the most abstract. The deepest and divinest idea that the mind of man can think is the idea of personality, and it finds a food in Christ that no abstraction can give.

Christianity, then, in giving us a Christ who is the person of truth, is not less intellectual than the faith which deals in the abstractions of eternity and infinity. It is a vastly more intellectual religion; and that is its power. It is the person in the truth that is the power in the truth. Truth is powerful as it is personal. Truth is weak and transient as it is abstract. Abstract ideas of truth or justice or morality have little power over men's lives, because there is little personality in such ideas. Their power is in proportion to the personality that is behind them. It is not because men have gotten hold of truth that they have done great things, but it is the truth that has gotten hold of men that has made heroes and martyrs and saints. That is Christ saying, "Follow Me."

You feel the force of what I say about the power of truth coming from the person in the truth whenever you go to the men who have worshiped truth. The moment you come up to one of these heroes, the men who have hazarded their lives for the cause of truth, the men who have suffered for truth, who have made the pursuit of truth their very meat and drink, then you feel how impossible it is that such men should have followed an abstraction. They were following a person in the truth. They could not see it, but there was a hidden Christ who called them through their science or their philanthropy. When a man follows truth with all the passion of a soldier for his captain, it is only a question of time in this world or the next when his heart finds Christ the leader for all seekers after truth.

Truth is real as it is personal; truth is unreal as it is abstract. The depth of truth is the important matter; not the mere breadth, but the depth, because that discloses the personality in the truth. It is not the size of a painting, but the art in a painting, we look for. We ask for depth in truth, not mere comprehension. And because deep truth is always personal truth, incarnate truth, therefore the discovery of truth is always less a matter of search than of discipleship. We speak of men who pursue truth, but truth has always pursued men more. There is a heart and a person back of truth that yearns to disclose itself. Men have always felt that truth flashed itself out to them. A man does not really discover truth, but truth discovers a man. The law of gravitation waited for Newton, and the doctrine of evolution waited for the great men of our day who should bring their devotion and discipleship. Truth is crowding on us today. How vastly more there is to learn than we have the patience or the discipline to receive! Every museum, every laboratory, every observatory, has far more material on hand for the discovery of truth than it is able to study and digest. Truth is knocking at our doors because the love of God is impatient to make itself known. Truth is besieging us because the Son of God is aflame with the desire to make known the Father. The wealth of thought and discovery that comes from all the quarters of the globe serves only to make us feel how precious is Christ, who is the living bread.

God made our souls to follow a leader. A man whose soul was once struck off from the eternal die of the Son of man is by nature a follower. He follows when he tries to learn the secrets of nature. He follows when he sets the laws which govern the land. He follows through his duty, through his pleasure, through his business, and through his grief. What a man can do he only knows when he sees the kindling eye of Christ. All that is good in us flows out to all that is good in Christ. Christ does not drive us, but He draws us. He is the one steady influence in the world that is gradually taken up into our lives and wrought out in all our experience. When a man falters, or it is dark, or he is smitten with the chill of loneliness, or his sacrifice seems cruel, or his strength begins to fail in the shortening days, then if he can only hear his Lord say, "Follow Me," he is at peace. Nothing but that voice can hold him. Indeed, it is only Christ, whose soul was transparent enough and simple and strong enough in its own perfect obedience, that dares say, "Follow Me." You do not dare say, "Follow Me." You do not dare say to your child, your servant, or your friend, "Follow Me." You warn men away from your own example, with its sins and its sorrows and its disobedience. But Christ says, with a voice that goes reverberating down through depth after depth of a man's nature, "Follow Me."

O men and women, come, follow Him. Follow Christ your Lord through every moment of your day, through your work and through your prayers, through your cares and your plans and your hopes. Follow Him with your passionate desire to know the truth; follow Him with your pains and fears and despair and failure; follow Him into peace and light. Do not be afraid that Christ will ever be less to the world than the incarnate truth. Christ is for all ages and for all nations truth's one clear call. All life takes its meaning from Him who is the source of life. In discipleship to Him the infinite passion of the human heart at last finds its outlet. We cannot be at rest until we rest in Him; we cannot be happy until we satisfy that deepest craving of our hearts to follow our Lord. While we sit, like Matthew, at the gate of the world's traffic, nursing all sorts of vague dreams and speculations, He, the Son of man, who owns our lives, who is our Lord, is standing before us saying, " Follow Me." Now Matthew arose and followed Him, and God grant that you and I this day and forever after may rise and follow Him.

JESUS ONLY

St. Matt. xvii. 8.

And when they had lifted up their eyes, they saw no man, save Jesus only.

JESUS ONLY

PETER and James and John, the chosen companions of the Lord, had gone up with Jesus into a high mountain apart. There a very wonderful thing happened, for suddenly our Lord was transfigured before them. That heavenly nature of our Lord, which was habitually hemmed in and concealed behind the veil of His human flesh, seemed now to shine through Him and burst on the astonished gaze of the apostles. More than this, there appeared also on each side of the Lord the flying forms of the great Jewish leaders, Moses and Elijah, adoring Him. Moses and Elijah were the great personalities of Jewish history, and it was common belief that when Messiah came He would confirm the law of Moses on the one hand, and fulfil the prophecy of Elijah on the other. There were some even who believed that Elijah would himself be born again as the Messiah. It seemed then to the disciples, in that moment of transfiguration, that they saw their Master acknowledged by the two great

Jewish prophets, who before their very eyes came and did homage to the Lord, and that henceforth there could be no doubt as to His being the Messiah. But while Peter, always the spokesman among the apostles, tried to speak, "a bright cloud overshadowed them: and behold a voice out of the cloud, which said, This is My beloved Son, in whom I am well pleased; hear ye Him." And the disciples fell on their faces filled with fear, until our Lord came and touched them and said, "Arise, be not afraid." And when they lifted up their eyes the vision was gone, and the air was still again, and the prophets had disappeared. Nothing now interrupted the familiar scene which they had looked down upon all their life, the same fields and roadways and hillsides and streams. A moment before it had all been blotted out by a divine vision. They hardly dared to look again at their Master after they had seen such a sublime change come over Him. They hardly dared to think what would greet their eyes next, after these heroic figures came out of heaven hovering around Him, and the voice from heaven confirming Him. Yet when they lifted up their eyes, they saw no man, save Jesus only.

The vision of the transfiguration was something which all their training had taught the disciples to expect. For an instant they saw before them what the whole nation hungered and prayed for, a prince of heaven strong enough to confound this world. For an instant they saw the divine person who was the Lord, to whom the prophets bowed and yielded homage. They were prepared instantly to follow such a Christ; they knew the whole nation was ready to follow such a Christ. For an instant it seemed as though everything was done and gained; all that men hoped for was at hand. But when they lifted up their eyes, they saw no man, save Jesus only; in an instant again it had all shrunk up to this. Instead of all the glory being given, all the prophecy being fulfilled, all the triumph being won, they had given to them only a hint, a glimpse, a shadow, and then began all the terrible, hard struggle to make it real. Instead of a Messiah coming down in the clouds of glory, overawing His enemies and smiting asunder His adversaries, separating with one imperious gesture the goats from the sheep, they lifted up their eyes, and saw no man, save Jesus only. There was everything before them yet to do. There were before them still all the laborious journeys, all the weariness, all the denial, all the persecution; there was before them still the treachery of the rabble, the shame of the cross, the utter blackness of dismal failure, before they could hope to bring in the kingdom of Christ.

You and I, brethren, can understand now that our Lord could come in no other way to help us; He had to come to us as Jesus only. He had to come as a man, and live among men as a man, and understand human tears and pains as a man, and suffer as a man, and as a man to die, before we could realize the wonder of the love of God. The wonder of God's love is that He could give His Son to take on Him the nature of a man. He had to be incarnated for that; He had to come down as Jesus only, and be accepted on man's plane until He should prove Himself by suffering and death the Christ of God. Is it not wonderful to see the depth of the wisdom and the penetration of Christ? Our Lord seems the wisest, the boldest, the sanest, the noblest of mankind. The saints of this world are sometimes trivial and sentimental, but our Lord never more or less than infinitely strong. The soldiers of this world are sometimes reckless and foolhardy, but He never more or less than bold. The thinkers of this world sometimes seem far-fetched and theoretic, but He never more or less than profound. The reformers of this world sometimes seem self-willed and egotistic, but He never more or less than self-effacing. Christ the Lord was great enough to meet the hardest test. An angelic king coming in the clouds would have endured no tests; no one would have dared to have put him to the proof; but our Lord was so divine, so strong, so sure of Himself, that He gave up all that might keep Him away from men, and came down to earth, and was born of Mary, and was subject unto His parents, and when He was thirty years old He went forth and called His disciples and preached the love of God in the kingdom of the Son; but when men lifted up their eyes, they saw no man, save Jesus only.

Christ did not come to the world in His glory; He came as Jesus only, and rose from earth transfigured by all that He was faithful in here. If I may speak in a human way, our Lord earned His Messiahship. He did not come to earth and assume divine power, but He lived His life so as to reveal it. When He went away, then He stood revealed. Our Lord, like all of earth's greatest men, was more anxious to seem real to men than to seem imposing or mighty. Reality was the thing He aimed at first, and accordingly the Christian religion is the most real of all faiths; the one having most to do with the facts; the one most closely reasoned out; the one most charged with the actual experience of human life. In the creed of the church there are no theological fancies, no pious generalities, no religious theories, but the plain statements of the life of Jesus only. The creeds that men have made for themselves may be full of an uncertain mass of views about predestination and damnation and inspiration; the creeds of men may be so full of medieval notions and ordinances, and so formidable, that one hardly dare think of what manner of Christ it may be who lays such an incubus on men; but the creed that has come down to us almost from the lips of the apostles is full of Jesus only.

Now men make the same mistake to-day as the disciples. They begin by trying to believe in the Trinity instead of first getting a practical, vital faith in Jesus only. Christ came first as a man, and we must first believe in Him as a man, and leave it to Him to make that faith shine with the mystery of an incarnate God. We can safely leave it to Him to show in good time how it needed all that awful stoop from the throne of God to the arms of the Virgin Mary to reveal the infinite compassion of God. Oh, why do we torture ourselves into a belief in something that we cannot understand, instead of first concentrating our whole heart on Jesus only, absorbing Him into our hearts and lives, and leaving Him to prove Himself all that seems dark and strange? All that we need for faith is Jesus only. It is very simple; real faith is always very simple— very hard, but very simple. We have only to begin as Christ began. If we will only think enough about Christ as a man, there is no fear but He will lead us on to cry, as Thomas at last cried, "My Lord and my God." There is some one here, perhaps, who is unable to accept Christ as the divine Son. Can you not accept Him as Jesus only, and leave to Him to prove all the rest? Can you not accept Him as the Friend and Helper and Master, and leave Him to make known in good time all that there is besides? Christ wants you more than your homage. The homage of men is nothing to the everlasting Son of God, though it makes all the world sweeter and stronger and purer when they yield that homage to their Lord. Let Christ have only the beginnings of your faith, give Him a mere standing place in your thought and the mere threshold of your heart, and leave it to Him to enable you "to comprehend with all saints what is the breadth and the length and the depth and the height, and to know the love of Christ which passeth knowledge, that ye may be filled with all the fullness of God."

Brethren, it is the simplicity of Christ that keeps some of us from making Him the power of our lives. We are tempted to shrink back when we find it is no wonderful dream of heaven and earth dissolving into a cloud of angels about the blazing form of Christ. Why, if I could preach such a Christ there would not be one of us, no, not the most careless, no, not the most world-hardened and ungrateful, who would not fall down and worship Him; but when we preach Jesus only, Jesus, the simple figure far back in the great years, though all the world of time is slowly wheeling around Him as the center on which all turns,— howbeit, only the angels of God can see that it is so,—men halt and are cold and put Him off, and Christ bleeds on the cross. We ask men to come and accept Christ, and feel His Spirit move in them and strengthen them for anything in this world or the next; but when they try to do just what we say, then the splendid vision of a Messiah passes away and there is Jesus only. There is only a man whom we are to live like, in whose steps we are to walk, whose commandments we are to keep. That does not seem at all like the inspiring face we first set out to follow. I ask you to receive Christ and yield your life to Him. What does it mean? Nothing that is in the least imposing or startling or moving, but everything that is brave and faithful and painstaking. It means to be baptized in His name, and become a member of Christ's church, and to come and receive the communion, and to lead a new life, and to repent of one's sins, and to live in charity among all men. I wonder I dare to say all that; it must seem so mean and trite and commonplace. You think you would like to lead a religious life, and you find it is a very tiresome task of prayer and duty, ordering your life in a certain way, curbing your temper, fighting your appetites, giving offerings that are real sacrifices, and not the mere alms you would never miss, and it seems hard and unfeeling and repelling. The light is suddenly all gone out of the vision, and there is the hard earth again and all the weary work of this earth; and yet all that is the only kind of foundation for a faith that will last. It takes *all the depth and the drudgery* and *the seriousness* of a life, it takes all the *downright earnestness* of a life, to make a faith. Nothing but a heart that is tremendously in earnest will acquire faith. Fine fancies do not make a religion, or pious talk, but the daily ordering of a whole life in loyalty to Jesus Christ. That is the faith in Jesus only, and out of that loyalty everything needful comes at last. We can do without a great deal if we are living a life of silent loyalty to Jesus only; we can endure to be beaten and tossed and disappointed, and we can go on and remain strong. The men who have hidden their lives with their Lord long enough to be absolutely cleansed from vanity and self-importance and self-seeking and the desire to rule have been the men content to follow Jesus only.

THE PRIVILEGE OF POWER

St. John XIII. 3-5.

Jesus knowing that the Father had given all things into His hands, and that He was come from God, and went to God; He riseth from supper, . . . and took a towel, and girded Himself, . . . and began to wash the disciples' feet.

THE PRIVILEGE OF POWER

OUR Lord excites in men a loyalty that does not arise out of their gratitude merely or out of their love merely, but from their sense also of His magnanimity. He always bore Himself in such a great way. Besides the innocence of Jesus, besides the compassion of Jesus, besides His strength, His heroism, or His tenderness, there is the magnanimity of Jesus. Here, at the Last Supper, "knowing that the Father had given all things into His hands, and that He was come from God, and went to God; He riseth from supper, . . . and took a towel, and girded Himself, . . . and began to wash the disciples' feet." For a moment one doubts whether these things belong together; one wonders whether the writer of the gospel was not hurried into putting these things together because he was nearing the awful climax of the redemption. But no, there it is, the calmest spot in all the Bible. Jesus, knowing that the Father had given all things into His hands, was great enough to assume nothing and to become the servant of all. Because "He was come from God, and went to God," He made Himself the least of those who followed Him. How sweet it is to repeat that over and over again! He became a servant *because* the Father had put all things into His hands; He humbled Himself *because* He came from God, and went to God. Because He was so great, He could be so simple and gentle and unassuming. Because all power in heaven and earth was His, He could lay aside His garments, and with a towel gird Himself, and could wash the disciples' feet.

Nothing could demean our Lord, because He was so great in Himself. His was a nature without resentment or retaliation or self-importance. He was in every moment of His life great. He was great when He stood up in the familiar synagogue before those who knew Him only as Jesus the carpenter's son, and He was great in His answers to those who tried to entrap Him by their malicious questions. He was great when He stood before Pilate. He was so great on the cross and in the hour of His humiliation that the Roman centurion who watched Him die said, "Truly this man was the Son of God." Our Lord might humble Himself to the lowliest service and to the meanest condition, but it served only to bring out more clearly the essential elevation of His soul.

Men have always sought in the leader whom they followed not only courage and power and resource, but those leaders who have carried the multitude in adoring loyalty have been magnanimous men—men of a large mold, men of breadth and greatness of heart. It is not enough to love one's leader, but the real leader must inspire in one a great moral respect. You want to feel in the men whom you follow an elevation of character, a soul superior to every kind of small dealing. Such a magnanimity men felt in Julius Cæsar, although Cæsar was a man of grave defects; Charlemagne was such a man; Lord Nelson and Washington were such—men of the great heart. Even grave faults and sins have been forgiven the favorite leaders of men, but they must be large-minded and large-hearted men; that is the character that we love most in our human heroes and leaders and captains.

Now this character of magnanimity our Lord shares with all lesser heroic and sought-after men. Our Lord is everything that any earthly hero is, and all heaven besides. His nature was as open as the day and as pervasive as the air. Everything there was in Him went out to everything in men and brought Him nearer to human trouble and infirmity and sin. Nothing in Him could ever be a barrier to any cry or prayer. Because He had all things put in His hands, He did not draw off in seclusion or make it a wall of privilege behind which He might shelter Himself, but every element of His power our Lord used to bring Him nearer to men and to share more of their lives. He never had to save Himself or protect Himself, but because all things were given into His hands, and because He came from God, and went to God, therefore He bowed Himself to the humblest of all tasks, that of washing His disciples' feet.

How differently we see men act in the world, often, who have some unusual ability or strength or means or position! How instinctively we see some men use their advantages to shut themselves away from their fellow-men! Almost the first thing that occurs to the man who has met with some rare fortune, or has won some marked success, is that there is something *now* he will not have to endure any longer. He will not *now* have to humble himself or submit to some galling indignity. He will *now* get away from this or that irksome duty. Pride, that never seems to be more than sleeping in human hearts, wakes up at every turn of fortune, and takes the lead, and rules all a man does. It is the constant peril of all culture that it tends to take men away from the great human needs and sympathies of life. But see our Lord, how He acted because all things were given into His hands, and because " He was come from God, and went to God." "He riseth from supper, . . . and took a towel, and girded Himself, . . . and began to wash the disciples' feet." Oh, how clear some things of this life seem after we have studied closely some one typical act or word of Christ! After that, who could hesitate for one instant to feel that the strength of such a Christ, the moral grandeur of such a Christ, was what this troubled world needed to live by?

By one act our Lord shamed out of men's hearts the whole world of sinful, black, and bitter pride; He reversed the world's way and the world's standard. The world boasted that, because of power, therefore one should oppress the weak; and because of talent, therefore one need not be innocent; and because of riches, therefore one should be hard. But Christ reversed all that, and we know Christ was right. Because a man has power, therefore he ought to protect the weak; because a man has talent, therefore he ought to be better than other men; because a man is cultivated, therefore he ought to show quicker sympathies. Do not make anything you have a reason for being selfish. Do as Christ did; make it a reason for being a servant. There was a time when the words "Noblesse oblige" made all the blood of all the nobility of Europe fire up. It meant that the high-born man must not save himself; it meant that if any one was to suffer, the humble man should not be that one; it meant that the prince must always be where the fight was thickest, the peasant where it was most safe. In the French Revolution the dainty women of the French court went out penniless, but they were the bravest souls in all France. Marie Antoinette went to the guillotine calm and composed, because she was a queen, but the wicked woman who was the king's favorite wept and wailed like a child. There were souls in those fiery days who felt it due themselves, because of their blood and their titles and their lands, to be never less than great.

It was our Lord who taught us that we men are strong not in our self-indulgence, but in our self-sacrifice; we are strong in our self-restraint, self-discipline, self-denial. The great joy of life comes in all that we share of others' lives. Whatever makes it possible to enter more into life, to know more of the world, to have a wider sphere of experience, to share more burdens, to do more work, to take part in more responsibilities, that is the real blessing of power; but whatever serves only to kill out of one the free, healthful sympathy for men of widely different conditions, that is our worst enemy. Because you have any advantage, show that it makes you more, not less, of a man, with broader, not narrower, interests.

Because you have intelligence and culture, show that you know how to suffer. Because you have high ideals, show that you can go without. Be great enough when it is necessary, in running the race of life, to come in last and not be cast down.

The Son of God was a magnanimous man. In our hearts we love a hero, a hero who is not merely strong, keen, or kind, but who is large-hearted. He is the hero whom we admire; he wins our adoring respect. Christ was so good, so pure, so wise, so bold, but then, too, He was made—may I say it in the words that we love to use of our mortal men?—He was made on such a large pattern. There was nothing in Him small or weak or fastidious. There is often something small in our saints and martyrs; there is often something weak or trivial in our human masters and teachers; but Christ was always the man of the great heart. Because all things were given unto Him, He left all and became poor. Because He came from God, and went to God, He laid aside all His glory, and came down to earth, and was made man, and was subject to Joseph and Mary. He went about among the sick and the helpless; He comforted the sorrowing; He took the little children up in His arms and blessed them; He spoke to that poor sinning woman of Samaria by the wellside, though she never dreamed of His condescension; He touched the loathsome leper; and He walked through all the towns of Galilee, footsore and unknown, because a prophet should not perish out of Jerusalem. He bore with the Pharisees, who tempted Him, and with the scribes, who sneered at Him; He washed the disciples' feet; He gave Himself as a sheep to the shearers, and as a lamb He was dumb, and He drew near the cross, though waiting till Peter should deny Him thrice. Then, when the redemption was won and a Saviour was given to the torn heart of men, and Christ had never once failed to be great or failed to be magnanimous, then a cloud received Him out of their sight, and He sat down in His ineffable glory at the right hand of God.

THE JOURNEY TO JERUSALEM

St. Mark x. 32.

And they were in the way, going up to Jerusalem; and Jesus went before them.

THE JOURNEY TO JERUSALEM

IT had begun to dawn on the disciples by this time what sort of an end our Lord was coming to. There had been a time when the kingdom of heaven seemed an easy victory. On every hand the crowds were waiting to receive them; men and women blessed God when Jesus drew near, and the sick and impotent folk sought only to touch the hem of His garment, and as many as touched were made whole of whatsoever disease they had. But things had now taken a different turn, and the disciples were experiencing a very unpleasant awakening. The way seemed ominously dark before them. So long as the message of Christ was proclaimed in Galilee it found a ready hearing. The people of Galilee were not the strictest of Jews, and they were only too ready to take up with new ideas and ways. But now that it was time to go to Jerusalem, where was the head and center of all, where the religious authorities were, where the temple worship was and all the established service of religion, the outlook became changed. It became plain that the reception of Jesus in Jerusalem would not be friendly. It was plain that the message of Jesus would not be acceptable to the Jews there, to the priests there, the scribes and the Pharisees, and that if Jesus persisted in going up at this time there was sure to be trouble, conflict, and the prison probably, and perhaps death.

So we read that as the disciples followed Jesus they were afraid. It seemed to them so unnecessary to go forward. It seemed to them that it would be better to keep away from Jerusalem and set up their party in some safe part of Palestine, and win a following, and strengthen their fellowship, and bide their time until the world came round to them. But when they looked at their Master, He seemed to them to hurry forward as though He was actually pressing toward His destruction with eager expectation. He knew all that was before them, for He had taken the Twelve and had told them what things should happen unto them. He knew the storm was gathering; He heard it muttering, and saw it just ready to break; and yet they saw Him going forward not sadly or despairingly, but as one who sprang up eagerly to claim His own. The disciples were amazed, and as they followed Jesus they were afraid. But Jesus pressed forward, strong, sure, steady, expectant, impetuous.

How very strange it seems that that relation of the disciples and our Lord has never been reversed! "They were in the way, going up to Jerusalem; and Jesus went before them." Jesus went before them in those days, and to-day, after so many years, it is the same. We are now in the way, going up to the Jerusalem of our time, and there is Jesus still ahead. The world is a vast affair, and its interests are innumerable, and the story of its advance is full of strange surprises; but the leadership of Christ is the only fact of the ancient world that has not been radically changed. A prophet in the days and the city of the Roman Emperor Augustus would have made little success in forecasting the ages as distant as ours. So many of the wisest prophecies have been falsified; so many of the most confident expectations have come to nothing; so many insignificant causes have become triumphant. Take all the interests of the world at the time of our Lord, all the thoughts, all the ideas, all the ambitions; perhaps the least to be considered of them all was that "they were in the way, going up to Jerusalem; and Jesus went before them"; and yet that least considered fact of those days is the one only key-note by which all subsequent ages have been described: "Jesus went before them." Jesus guides our feet to-day into the way of truth. He went before the ages that were dark and enlightened them. He went before the ages that were unlearned and He taught them. He went before the ages and the men who were fearful and He comforted them. We cannot tell the future of our age; we cannot tell the future of our country or know if it can weather the storms of her selfish factions and last on into new and other centuries; but this one fact we know: that we are being led on by some strange destiny somehow and somewhere; we are swept along in some mysterious pilgrimage of which we know nothing, save only that we are like the disciples, who " were in the way, going up to Jerusalem; and Jesus went before them."

We can look back and see how much wiser the Lord was than the disciples, who thought it better not to go up and tempt their fate in Jerusalem, but to go away and be a leader of a party, like any one of the thousand leaders who had set up standards of revolt, and flourished for a time, and then been defeated, and died forgotten. Our Lord went up to Jerusalem not to lead a party, but to redeem the world. He went up to Jerusalem to save men from their sins, to teach men how through suffering to attain peace, and how through great tribulation to enter the kingdom of heaven. He went up to Jerusalem to show that the secret of all joy and life was to press forward toward truth and right, no matter how it might hurt, and that the secret of all sin was to hold back and to try and save one's self, no matter what one might gain. Jerusalem meant peace to Christ, because He saw in it all that He might win through suffering, but it meant pain to the disciples, because they saw in it only what they dreaded. So "they were in the way, going up to Jerusalem; and Jesus went before them."

There is one feeling that no man can extinguish in him, and that is the feeling that his life is going forward, making for some goal. Every heart feels itself moving in the mysterious current. We cannot get rid of it. The more we think, the more vividly it stands out that we are tending toward something. The more we see and experience, only the more certain it becomes. There is not one of us who is not thinking what the future may bring forth. We cannot help those clouded thoughts; we cannot help peering forward and wondering whether it will all come out right, whether the problem will be settled, whether the burden can always be borne, whether the danger will disappear, whether some sudden succor will not come in to save us. Perhaps there is some one who does not know how he is ever going to meet what to-morrow will bring. But "they were in the way, going up to Jerusalem; and Jesus went before them." Jesus goes before; He leads the way; He knows it all. Christ is always the Lord of the march. He is as much the Lord of your journey as He was of that journey to Jerusalem. Just as He pressed forward there, not fearfully, not wonderingly or frightedly, like the disciples, but eagerly, confidently, resolutely, so He presses forward with us now. Remember you are always behind Christ. "Jesus went before them." Go meet your care or your danger or your trouble just as though you saw Him vividly ahead of you. When the disciples saw in His face that look of intense expectation, then it was all different for them and Jerusalem became the battle-ground of their life. Is not that the divine truth for our lives? The very thing you and I are dreading most is the battle-hour of our lives, the chance to prove ourselves to ourselves. Christ said so; Christ showed it was so. He tells you you do wrong to look on that work you have to do, that danger you have to meet, that loss you have to overcome, as something hostile to your life. No; these things belong to you and to me; they are part and parcel of our souls. You cannot separate me from my problem and I not be less of a man. I and my problem go together. You cannot turn me aside from the hour of my danger and I not be less of a man. That doubt or problem or disappointment is not a thing outside me, but something that is bound up with my being. It is *my* doubt, *my* problem, *my* disappointment. It is something that belongs to me to meet and to struggle with and to conquer. That was the light and the sweetness and the serenity which the disciples saw in the Lord's face as " they were in the way, going up to Jerusalem; and Jesus went before them." It seemed to our Lord sweet to go to Jerusalem, sweet to contend with the fanatics of Jerusalem, sweet to be haled before Pilate, sweet to climb the cross; for it had been written of the Son of man that so it should be, and Christ the Son of man must come to His own.

You and I would never of ourselves have chosen to go up to Jerusalem, but Christ knows that when we rise up and follow Him there, then our lives begin to deepen; when we begin to suffer, then we begin to be wise; when we feel the burden bow our backs, then we begin to know what strength is. It is the stricken soul that is driven to God for shelter. No man ever yet found his powers who had not learned how to use them through all disturbance, danger, fear, trouble, or grief. No man ever possessed his talent who had not learned to use it in all its perfection even when his heart was sick and sore and aflame. In going to Jerusalem Christ is always leading us to find ourselves.

There is that last dread journey. Must I not

make that alone? Suppose God should call me to-night, summon me to leave earth and to appear before Him,—me, yes, me,—summon me to die, to lay this warm, pulsing body down, and leave it cold and still and dead, and die. Was there ever anything so unheard of, so tragic, so terrible? It must have been easier for others to die; it could not have been so hard for them to be spared; they could not have been so unprepared. Is not that the way we think of ourselves in connection with death? Each one thinks, "How can I ever endure the thought of death coming to claim me as he has claimed so many others? How can I ever yield and follow?" But most men die gently and peacefully, as though each one felt himself gently drawn from earth and carried along in the train of those who " were on the way, going up to Jerusalem; and Jesus went before them."

"Jesus went before them." Brethren, that is your world. That is the world which the blessed feet of Christ have touched till it thrilled to its center. That is the life you are engaged in, with fears and worries and mistakes and sorrows and losses and death. The great wonderful thing about this world's history is that Jesus leads the way. We shall never outgrow our Lord. The times will change; the nations will pass and be born; new visions of unthought-of things will come. Will our Lord ever fall behind at last in the great pilgrimage? Will the time ever come when men will look back on Him instead of forward to Him, and will refer to Him kindly but condescendingly, and point out here and there how Jesus was weak, and failed to meet human needs, and how His whole point of view of life is transcended? Ah! it is not that which makes the Christian fearful. If the Christian had any fear it would be that our Lord's gospel should come in time to seem so far above him, so dangerously out of man's reach, as to be a mere dream of God. But is not that the surest proof of Christ the Son of God, and that He will keep His promise, and be with us always, "even unto the end of the world"?

"And Jesus went before them." There are times when that is all we wish to know; when it is best not to see the world at all, nor the things that are in it, nor its tenderest associations or ties, but only to see the one great overshadowing fact that Jesus goes before us. This world has many precious things; it rings with truth and courage, and beauty is strewn along the way; but there are dark things in the world, dreadful things, things to fill one with a wild horror and doubt of God, until we look away from it, forget everything, turn away from everything, know nothing, see nothing, except that exultant face of Christ as He leads us down the path of the heavenly Jerusalem. Let me write very deeply into the fleshly tablets of my heart that as " they were on the way, going up to Jerusalem, . . . Jesus went before them."

PRAYER

St. Luke vi. 12, 13.

And it came to pass in those days, that He went out into a mountain to pray, and continued all night in prayer to God. And when it was day, He called unto Him His disciples: and of them He chose twelve, whom also He named apostles.

PRAYER

THE scribes and the Pharisees were very angry at Jesus, and they watched Him closely to destroy Him. They were not softened or pacified when they saw His acts of healing; it only angered them the more, because they realized how dangerous a man they had to deal with. Our Lord lived and wrought in the midst of contention and misunderstanding. All the time sour and envious glances were bent on Him, and while He taught that God so loved the world that He gave His only begotten Son, that whosoever believed in Him should have everlasting life, there smoldered in many hearts the fires of hate, that only waited to break out and consume Him. Through it all, however, our Lord kept Himself calm and composed, alive to all that was working around Him, but never disturbed or angry or bitter or railing. What was it that enabled Jesus to live under provocation, continually harassed by petty persecution, continually set upon with questions designed to trip Him up, thrust out of His own city, with His own disciples disputing among themselves who should be greatest in the kingdom of heaven, conspired against, and at last betrayed by one of the Twelve? How was it that our Lord bore Himself strong and pure and kind and tender and spotless through it all? It was the way our Lord restored and fortified Himself by long-sustained prayer. When the Jews saw how Jesus had healed the man with the withered hand on the Sabbath day, "they were filled with madness, and communed one with another what they might do to Jesus." Besides, it was necessary now for our Lord to choose His twelve disciples. For all time His church was to be known by these twelve men. Nothing could be more important or carry more consequences of good or evil with it. The fate of the Christian church hung on His choice. He might well have hesitated, finding Himself in the midst of enemies. The scribes and the Pharisees were filled with madness at Him and looking around to see how they might take Him. For such a crisis our Lord prepared Himself by spending the night in prayer. Continuing prayer was our Lord's preparation for trial. "It came to pass, . . . that He went out into a mountain to pray, and continued all night in prayer to God."

Jerusalem slept while our Lord "continued all night in prayer to God"; Jerusalem, whose doom had sounded, was fast in sleep. Herod on his tottering throne, surrounded by those who only waited their chance to avenge a father or a son's murder, was asleep. The priests, whose temple was soon to be razed to the ground so completely that not one stone was left upon another, were asleep. The populace slept, who were soon to be ingulfed in the awful terrors of a siege, where starving women devoured even their own children. But the Son of man, who was to begin His many journeys over all Galilee, who was to be tried by sordid followers, hated by those whom He exposed, about whom the crowds were to throng till He could get no rest, and who was at last to be overborne and betrayed and mocked and crucified, He who had all this before Him when the day broke, "went out into a mountain to pray, and continued all night in prayer to God."

We cannot help wondering why our Lord prayed so. Why should *He* have continued all night in prayer to God, who was Himself God, the divine Son, made man, the express image of the Father, to whom all power in heaven and on earth was given, by whom all things were made that were made? He was God, and He was man. He, the only begotten Son of God, came down from heaven and took on Him the nature of man. He became not *a* man, but *man*. He took human nature on Him. God the Father did not merely create man, but He gave His only begotten Son to be man, to enter into every difficulty and fear and labor and pain that man has to bear. His divine nature and His human nature did not destroy each other. He remained, and He remains now, perfect God and perfect man. He was really in the bosom of the Father from all eternity, but He really prayed. He could have commanded the very stones to become bread, yet He continued all night in prayer to God. He could have summoned legions of angels to His rescue, but yet as man, too, He felt all the yearning, the pain, the passion, the torments, the fears, that make men here on earth pray. He prayed because He was a Son; because the heart of a son seeks the heart of a father. Our Lord's prayer was the turning of a Son to His Father. He did not pray to be set free from the purpose of redemption, or to turn back on the way He had come to save man, but, as a child, to be restored and strengthened by hiding Himself in His Father's bosom. To keep on, and not to falter or to be turned aside, to put difficulties in their right place, and finally to beat down Satan under His feet, He prayed. There was perfect faith in our Lord's prayer, perfect purity of heart, perfect sincerity of purpose, perfect resignation to God's will, perfect innocence, combined with the frail and halting body. His spirit was absolute and sure and sinless, but the flesh was weak; perfect in His desire and aim and will, and weak only in the body through which these things make themselves felt.

Our Lord, who was all that, spent the whole night praying. To continue all night in prayer to God was His preparation for the most important act in setting up the kingdom. The clearness, the judgment, the insight, and the sincerity which He used in choosing the twelve captains of Christendom came in that night of prayer. Most of the hard things in life we know before they come on us. There is often time, if we had the mind, to get ready for them. Now we often get ready for a hard labor, or a great strain of endurance, or a vexation, or a season of pain, by easing things up generally, by extra indulgence, and by relaxing our usual care of ourselves. Our Lord's example, however, is the better. He continued all night in prayer to God. If you have to make a decision on which a great deal depends and about which you fear to make a mistake, do what your Lord did: spend a long time in uninterrupted prayer and meditation. I say a long time not because we have a very long story to tell God, or because it is necessary that our petition should be very long drawn out, and said over and over again like a teasing child, before God will hear, but because we need to be filled with Christ's purity and courage. We need to spend a long time because it takes a long time to change the whole temper of a man and to make one's soul free from everything that God cannot countenance in a trusting child of His. We need to hold our souls up to God as we hold a pitcher at the spring and wait until the clear, cold water has filled the vessel to the brim. We have to wait long, with the world shut out, with our mind concentrated on our Lord, filling ourselves quite full of the spirit of obedience, quelling all the risings of rebellion. We have to take the time to be quite composed, to have all our impatience quite subdued, all our bitterness overcome, all our hard feelings softened, and all the fever of our souls cooled down into a state in which we can judge calmly, think temperately and accurately, and be masters of ourselves. We have to spend a long time, if possible, not doing another thing but pray, if possible by ourselves, if possible on our knees; not because it takes a long time to make God listen or to attract God's attention, to soften and change His mind toward us, but because it takes a long time to change our whole frame of mind toward God. In meeting our trials, in bearing grief, in enduring hard things, everything depends on our being in the right frame of mind. It takes quiet and devotion and plenty of time to change rebellion into obedience, and a sense of smarting into a sense of trust. And when it is not possible to let the hands be idle or to go by ourselves and fall on our knees, it is possible to spend the same long time in prayer by drawing the mind in to itself, by abstracting one's self as much as the hands will allow, and making the same long preparation by continuing prayer.

Our Lord continued all night in prayer as a preparation for the great crises and emergencies of life. How do we prepare ourselves for our trials and crises and hard tasks? I fear it will be a shame to you, as it is to me, to think how differently we do our preparation. Let us be honest with ourselves, brethren. How little continuing prayer we give! How short and quick and curt our prayer is! How soon over, how hurried through, how little attended to, and all to give place to how much anxiety, how much fretting and worrying! How excitedly we drive about, how distractedly we do things, how flurried we become, how unable we are to see what is really important and what is secondary! How we nurse all the bitter reflections that spring up in our minds, how angry we feel toward those who have injured us or brought us to our trouble, or who are not doing what we think they ought to do! How we quicken the memories of wrongs and slights, how we let ourselves become irritable and suspicious and bitter, and filled with rancor and envy and complaining! What a preparation for the breaking day! Then, some day, there is the great account to give. We are called to die. Men have gone on living as though there were no such thing as death, while it comes to one or another about them constantly. Men live without realizing that some day they themselves must die, but there has been no thought to prepare one for what death means, or what happens after death, or whether there be any hereafter. But suddenly, in the midst of men's thoughtlessness, death comes—not now the death of a neighbor, but your death, my death. You and I stop and we are seen no more; our place is empty. We are no longer seen on the streets, at our business, around our fireside. It is about us that men are talking and saying their kind or their careless words, according as we have made others feel that we cared for something besides ourselves. We are become memories and names, and our places filled, and our goods deeded, and the great world goes on, and now and then only we are recalled in connection with some story or incident. We are no longer here, but where shall we be, and how will it be with us then, and how will what we prize most now and think most about now seem to us then? We shall have time to think of our souls then, for the day of eternity has dawned and God has called us to spend it with Him. Shall we be shriveled up with shame then, or shall we press forward with a soul satisfied at last to cry, as we throw ourselves down at His feet, "My God and my Lord"?

There are hard things that we have to meet, but if we fit ourselves to meet them they bring a certain kind of exhilaration. The work you do that you are perfectly well able to do, perfectly skilled and disciplined to do, has a real enjoyment about it for a healthy mind. So there is actually something akin to that in the burdens and trials and troubles which we have fully prepared ourselves for. We go through them with a kind of exhilaration and glow. When our Lord on that eventful morrow called unto Him the disciples, and of them chose twelve, whom also He named apostles, how filled with sublime confidence He was! How sure and certain He was as He moved among them and laid His hand on James and John and Peter and Matthew and Bartholomew! He knew what sort of foundation-stones He had set there to build the temple of the living God. He knew they were not perfect, but they were men that could wait for their God. They might seem to wrangle for the first place, but when the time came they laid down their lives for the Lord Jesus. Our Lord knew He was making no mistake in James and John and Simon Peter and Bartholomew. The calm of that night of prayer went into the choice of the Twelve. Now, so when we enter on the trials and anxieties and sorrows for which we have made long and careful preparation by prayer, bringing our hearts into perfect obedience to God, we too are full of confidence and equanimity and calm and cheer. We have on us the whole armor of God; we are not unprepared. The weak man is always unprepared; unprepared for his task, for his load, for his sickness, for his sorrow, for his death. The strong man is always prepared; he has gotten ready for the things that take other men by surprise. What you most admire in some men, the sureness of touch with which they work, the clearness of mind with which they think, that kind of flame of truth with which they speak,—all that seems so simple and pure and strong and fills you with wonder,— came from the long, continuing, prayerful preparation. There were long hours of stillness behind the victories or the triumphs which you and I see; there were long and unseen struggles and strokes of discipline. They hid their lives away with God, driving their thoughts back to the great central convictions of their soul, thinking long and hard about their duty, pondering long and hard over their sorrows, bowing down in contrition at their sins; but when it was day they went out among men, and they seemed head and shoulders above other men. They were not easily disconcerted; their nerves were like steel wire; their brains worked swiftly, accurately, and absolutely true. They did not come from hours of weak self-pity, or self-gratification, or repining, or saving themselves. They came from following their Lord, as in those days " He went out into a mountain to pray, and continued all night in prayer to God."

LENT

St. Matt. iii. 1.

In those days came John the Baptist, preaching in the wilderness of Judea.

LENT

OUR Lord said that "among them that are born of woman there hath not arisen a greater than John the Baptist: notwithstanding, he that is least in the kingdom of heaven is greater than he." John the Baptist was the last of a long line of Jewish prophets. He felt himself that he belonged to a race that was passing away. He felt himself that he closed up one age of prophecy, while he saw in our Lord the beginning of another and a far more wonderful age. One day, when St. John saw Jesus as He walked, he said to his disciples, "Behold, the Lamb of God!" He felt in our Lord a peace and gentleness and holiness so much purer and higher than his burning and almost ferocious righteousness that he said to his disciples, "He must increase, but I must decrease."

That passionate expectation of a Messiah, which had existed ever since the time of Abraham and which makes the Jewish people the most remarkable of all the nations of the earth, had at last culminated in him who came in those days preaching in the wilderness of Judea, and saying, "Repent ye; for the kingdom of heaven is at hand." St. John came now, charged with all that had been dreamed and despaired of and then longed for from generation to generation. It may seem strange, therefore, that when it had been revealed to him that the coming of the Lord was near, instead of taking his place in Jerusalem and in the temple, where his father sacrificed, he should leave home and kindred and altar and seek to hide himself in the wild country between Jerusalem and the Dead Sea. St. John might have sought his following in the streets of Jerusalem if he had thought of his own reputation or influence as a prophet. But he felt that Christ's coming made everything else dwindle into insignificance. He felt that nothing that man might do or might not do could hasten or retard what was determined in the wisdom of almighty God. One heart utterly on fire with its obedience was a better preparation for Christ than a whole nation merely aroused and curious. Accordingly he turned away to brood in solitude. St. John is one of the best-known figures of the world. Every one is familiar with his appearance. A camel's-hair garment clothed him; the locusts and wild honey fed him. When the crowds came out and asked him, "What shall we do?" he said,

"Repent ye; for the kingdom of heaven is at hand."

St. John belongs to a class of men whom we may call the world's great convincers of sin. They were men who made their fellows realize the holiness of God and how great sinners they were in the sight of God. Isaiah and Jeremiah were such convincers of sin. St. Augustine was such a man and seemed ever to be consumed with the sorrow for his sin. St. Bernard had such an effect on men that Europe was swept from one end to another by the crusades which he preached. Savonarola was a John the Baptist of Florence in the fifteenth century. He worked on the Florentines until one day, in a passion of renunciation, they heaped up in a pile of incredible value books, pictures, musical instruments, jewels, articles of luxury and personal adornment, and burned them. Calvin was such a man, and ordered Geneva like a monastery. Jonathan Edwards in Northampton wrought on men and women so that they rushed from their meeting-houses shrieking with convulsions.

Very extravagant and absurd it seems to you and to me. It seems very unnatural for St. John to turn away from all the influence which he might have had as the son of Zacharias the priest, and become a solitary in the wilderness. But do we remember that something in men's hearts demanded just that kind of satisfaction? These men made God and His righteous judgments seem so real that in comparison the world and all it contained seemed unreal. Had you and I been in Florence at the time of Savonarola, or Geneva at the time of Calvin, or Northampton at the time of Edwards, and had we felt as keenly as they did the reality of God's law, we should have done the same.

St. John went into the wilderness because Christ seemed so near and real to him. He would not have his mind distracted from the one idea that possessed him. Whenever Christ becomes real to men it makes the world for a time seem to be unreal. When Christ becomes a living reality to a man, then, at least for a time, it throws the rest of his life into the shade. When Christ comes He makes of our ordinary lives a wilderness, because we can think of nothing but Him. It was not an accident, it was by a kind of moral necessity, that St. John went into the wilderness when he felt that the kingdom of heaven was at hand. The coming of Christ made all Judea seem a wilderness to St. John. Perhaps it seems strange to you that the season of Lent follows so soon upon Christmas. Perhaps it seems strange to you that hardly have we ceased to celebrate the birth of Christ, hardly have the bells of Christmas ceased to echo and the thoughts of Christmas ceased to stir our hearts, than it is all hushed in the somber shades of Lent. It seems like putting one's hand suddenly on a sweet and joyous bell that had sounded and stopping in an instant all vibration and tone. It is not an accident, however, but a deep necessity, that brings these two seasons so near together. That is the deep insight of the church. If Christmas has been a real birth of Christ, then it must make us reflect on the transitoriness of this world. When our Lord comes He dwarfs everything else, and Lent comes because our hearts must stop and feel what Christ is. There is some one who has looked on the Lenten season as though it were an arbitrary fancy, a mere medieval notion of repeating the forty days that our Lord spent in the wilderness; as though it were a relic of outgrown ideas and not really in accord with the interests of to-day. Can you not see now that it is not so? There could not be a Christmas without a Lent. There could not be a church thrilled through with the advent of Christ, and there not be immediately after a church sobered and watching and fasting and turning away from the world which Christ makes us see will come to an end.

You know how true an experience this is. A man learns of an act of great and quiet heroism, and it seems instantly to hush some of the clamoring desires within him. There was something that before he felt he could not do without, but now he feels he cannot bear to have. There are certain experiences and trials after which it seems somewhat sweet to be hard with ourselves. We feel as though we were more ourselves to go without, or to make extra effort, or to do more than is required of us. That is your wilderness following closely on Christ's coming. When Christ comes in some special way to my heart, then I cannot help the world shrinking to smaller proportions. If I could make you feel to-day Christ standing beside you and waiting to make you, oh, so strong with His strength, so confident, so full of love, would not the world seem to you less urgent, its pleasures less engrossing, its luxuries less necessary, its fashion less lasting? If our hearts were suddenly to fill up with the passionate loyalty to Christ, would not that make of our world, for a little time at least, a still wilderness, where we had time to think? That great anxiety of yours, would it not throb less fiercely in your heart? That great burden, would it not weigh less on your soul? Would not your fears be lightened up with hope?

On the other hand, if we want to get hold of Christ must we not make some special effort and hush the world for a time? Must we not keep it under and rise above it? Lent is the wilderness into which we may go to strengthen and purify our spiritual life. There are many men and women whose lives lack just that depth which a time of special prayer and self-denial gives. We all know that the power of a man is in proportion to the depth of his life, to all that lies behind what he says, to all the reserve force that he can bring into play. But that quality of depth can only come by going apart, by sober and solemn thought about one's self, by curbing one's desires at times, and by getting the mastery. Without that no man knows what his character is really worth. The power by which you really influence your friend, or win men's confidence, or awaken the adoring obedience of your children, comes from that wilderness where you keep a silent vigil with Christ. That lets you keep your character keyed up through sickness, through misfortune, through sorrow, and in the hour of death.

There are so many interests to-day that it seems as though men could not find the time to let religious ideas take real root in their hearts and grow there. Nothing will grow in a soil that is being continually turned over, and nothing will take root in a heart that has no time of silence and quiet and meditation. I am never without a fear lest sermons should defeat the very end for which they are given. These moral and religious ideas that we preach almost from our Lord's lips are throbbing with heroism and humanity; they fill one with exhilaration. But exhilaration does not last; it does not of itself bring obedience, which solves more problems and heals more heartaches than any other power of our souls. There is the greatest danger that we simply enjoy moral ideas as a kind of luxury of feeling, whereas luxury of feeling leads straight to downright insensibility. Yet, unless truth is taken into the soul and unless we stop long enough to ponder on it, to wrestle with it, to assimilate it, unless a man's soul has some wilderness like that wilderness of Judea where St. John came preaching, "Repent," into such a religious insensibility there is a great danger that we fall.

Faith, like every other human effort, requires time. It has been noted as a misleading idea of Americans that they think everything can be done by splendid spurts of energy. But all the spiritual results of man are done slowly. Poems are written slowly, pictures are painted slowly. Men toil long and silently over all of those achievements by which they throw a spell over their race. Faith too, the highest art of all, takes time. It takes a wilderness; it takes a Lent. Men imagine that faith will spring up in them when they hear a pat argument. Men think that some kind of spiritual prescription can be written out or put up, and that then all difficulties will vanish. But faith is the soul's health, and it takes quite as much time as the body for the recovery of its strength.

The most perplexing problem about human

life is that of making men see themselves as they really are. We are all the while taking ourselves for just the opposite of what we are. We imagine we are perfect in just the particulars in which we are really deficient, and we imagine we are deficient in just the qualities that are already overdeveloped. The man who is already too yielding thinks he ought to give way more, and the man who is quite obstinate thinks he ought to cultivate more determination. Very few men know what their weak points really are. How can we undeceive ourselves? How can we turn round on ourselves to see ourselves as every one else sees us? Why, by spending a great deal of time at a season with Christ, who will open our eyes. Men and women, this is a call to think about our souls. They are the most important thing for us to think about. They will last on forever. God meant them to grow, as they will if we attend to them. But does it not seem often as though our souls remained about the same, without growing a particle? They go on from year to year just as sinful, just as selfish, just as sordid, just as fearful, just as careless. One week only of dwelling on Christ with special effort would perceptibly broaden and deepen and strengthen them.

St. John the Baptist went into the wilderness to wait for the coming of his Lord. He wanted to concentrate his soul on Christ, so that he should not miss a moment of His coming or lose a syllable of what He said. That made him quick to see our Lord, although He came as a man of a totally different temper from St. John. That made him unfaltering when he rebuked Herod and Herod's sin. That made him die too. What our lives are pining for is inward power and inward vision. We are not rooted fast; we are doubtful and wavering, and our feet falter; but God, in His infinite mercy, points out to us how "in those days came John the Baptist, preaching in the wilderness of Judea."

GOOD FRIDAY

St. Mark xv. 39.

And when the centurion, which stood over against Him, saw that He so cried out, and gave up the ghost, he said, Truly this man was the Son of God.

GOOD FRIDAY

A ROMAN centurion had been stationed at the cross until our Lord should die. He was impatient for it all to be over, so that he might be free. But then began the strange transformation of that soldier's life. As he watched our Lord die an intense interest in that dying Saviour awakened within him. As he waited there he began to be profoundly moved and stirred. In that hour of weakness and collapse he saw not a sign of anything that was not genuine, strong, and true, but, on the other hand, he saw signs of a power that shone through and transfigured His weakness. It was the way in which our Lord died that made such a deep impression on the man who was familiar with the whole trade of death. It made that centurion believe just to see our Lord die.

How wonderful Christianity is, that, on whatever side it touches life, it seems so strong and convincing! Think of our Lord winning over this careless man just by the way in which He met His death! There is some one, perhaps, whom you are yearning to bring to the foot of the cross, and you are careful to point out all the signal things, all the comforting things, all the miraculous things in your religion. You dwell on its triumphs and its progress; you appeal to all that has been justified by time; but here is our Lord winning a believer in the hour of His defeat. We expect our Lord to win followers when He performed His miracles and when He preached to the people as never man spake before. We expect Him to extort even an unwilling belief from some of those who looked on breathless as He stood before Pilate, when even Pilate was moved and troubled. Who would have thought, however, that in the very way our Lord breathed out His last breath He should make there also His great appeal? Yet, "when the centurion, which stood over against Him, saw that He so cried out, and gave up the ghost, he said, Truly this man was the Son of God."

There is a sublime simplicity about this incident. Here for a moment Christianity is narrowed down to the two men—our Lord on the cross and the soldier keeping guard. Everything in the past is dead. His words have died away; His miracles are forgotten; His prophecies seem falsified; His disciples have all forsaken Him and fled. There is nothing to look forward to; there is only a man left to slowly breathe His life away; and Christ won. The centurion said, "Truly this man was the Son of God." What a singular conversion! What an awful moment in which to make a follower! I do not know of anything grander in all Christianity than this scene. Perhaps it seems grander to you that our Lord was transfigured on the mount; perhaps it seems grander to you that He fed the multitudes. To me it seems grandest of all in Christianity that my Lord in the hour of His failure and His humiliation made those who watched Him die believe on Him. He did not ask for men's belief because He could do miracles; He did not offer Himself to men's allegiance because He was infinitely wiser and better and stronger than any other one who ever lived. He offered Himself because He was infinitely more stanch and unfaltering and obedient to His Father's will. What He was with the disciples and the multitudes, that He was on the cross. It is what a man is when he has lost all that shows the real man; it is what a man can do without the world that makes men believe in him. When our Lord was stripped of everything that belonged to Him, defeated and forsaken, then, even in His death, He died like a God. It was enough for these soldiers to see our Lord die, and they believed on Him.

Now here is the stupendous example that our

Lord sets before us. How do men regard us when they see us fail and meet disappointment, and when sorrow comes, and when all that once inspired us is gone? Do we ever win a believer because of the way in which we bear these things? Men are constantly meeting their reverses or seeing the dreams of a lifetime dry up. You see men fall into great misfortune, and, alas! shelter themselves at any cost. You see men lose their property, and abandon their principles. They come into desperate straits, and twist their consciences. We often see such men let faith go, desert their church, neglect the sacraments, forget their Bibles, become cynical and cold, deny Christ, yes, deny the sincerity of all faith. Why? Because of anything the church has done? Because of any new facts or new light on God or the Bible? No; but because they have been plunged into misfortune; because their hearts are sick with envy; because they could not follow their Lord through sorrow and failure and affliction. But then look at your Lord on the cross. He is dying; He is wasting away in an awful agony of protracted pain. That glorious dream of a redeemed world has shrunk up to this sordid spectacle on the Mount of Calvary, an angry penalty under an angry sky. That is all that is left; but as the centurion watches our Lord in that dark hour he becomes a believer. "Truly," he said, as he sank back from the strain of watching the cross, "this man was the Son of God."

The centurion who was set there to guard our Lord was a plain man. He was not versed in books. His mind probably did not turn at all in the direction of spiritual things. He lived in Jerusalem and knew all that was going on, but he was not a man to be affected by our Lord's words. He did not have the ears to hear about the kingdom of heaven. The works that undoubtedly he saw our Lord do hardly concerned him; but when he saw our Lord die, then there awoke in that rough man of battle the wonderful essence of belief. Nothing else in all the world could have opened his heart but to see a man die for his truth. He saw Christ die, and he believed.

When you see a man take up his work again after his blow, calm and careful as before, suffering not a word of complaint or self-pity to escape him, permitting himself not the least act of indulgence, putting all his old-time faithfulness into his obligations, although his heart is dead, then you believe in that man just as the centurion believed in the Lord on the cross. There *are* men who can go up with our Lord on the cross and suffer and die with Him. Life to them is a post, which nothing can make them desert. If their own hopes are destroyed they show just the same fire and vitality in everything for which others are depending on them. We see these men lose, or fall behind, or meet grief, or surrender all they have been living for, and as we watch them our hearts fill with the wonder of the cross of Christ. These are the men who suffer without becoming cynical. They meet misfortune without becoming bitter. They see others enjoy what is denied to them and they have no envy. They bear trouble in such a way that the world about them seems richer and brighter. They bear grief in such a way that a whole household is filled with courage. When a man stands firm like that his life becomes wonderful to himself with new, strange, and rich meanings, and then straightway it becomes wonderful to all other men. They believe in him, because they see he measures his life not by what befalls him, but by the command of his Lord, who set him at his post.

There are men and women all about us who are just like this centurion. They can be brought to the cross of Christ only by seeing some one stake something for his faith, suffer something, endure something, go without something. There are men and women who do not care for any of our arguments for Christianity. They are not touched by the peace that falls on our hearts. But if they only see some one who bears his load because he believes in Christ, who meets his disaster and keeps his principles, then they understand. You might say a thousand fine words about your faith, but one simple act of fortitude for Christ's sake will carry conviction a thousand times deeper. O brethren, God forgive us Christian believers for all the shallowness and worldliness and selfishness and insincerity on account of which hungry hearts are turned away from Christ, the living bread. God forgive us for all the miserable weakness that we leave for an example to those who are growing up around us. I wonder if we realize, fathers and mothers, that there is no lesson that sinks down so deeply into a child's soul as that of a hardship borne bravely and lovingly or a sorrow borne with consecration. Children are at times the hardest and severest of all unbelievers. They have tasted the world just enough to see its folly and not enough to make allowances or to feel compassion. They seem utterly *impenetrable* to religious truth. The sweetest words of Christ fall on deaf ears. But they appreciate the man who is true when he is hit hard; they see Christ in the man who allows nothing to become an excuse for double-dealing, who keeps his heart pure, and who is content to be justified to his God. That is an argument that cannot be mistaken and that cannot be withstood.

Bring your *heroism* to Christ. Do not bring

Him the fidelity only that comes easy, but the fidelity that comes hard also. Do not bring Him the belief only that you were taught as a child, and you took on faith, but bring Him the belief that you have worked out in the experience of men, and that has been burned into you by the furnace of adversity. Give Christ the loyalty that you had after you had learned that the world could be cruel. Stand up for Christ with the convictions that you have had to struggle to keep. Men are watching us Christians all the time to see whether our religion is a matter of mere custom or personal advantage or respectability, or whether it is a strength to live by. Can you dare to lose with Christ? for every one must in some way or other lose. Can you dare to die with Christ? for certainly every one must, in God's good season, suffer and die. That was the kind of test our Lord met and satisfied. He showed that the slightest word, the weakest act, of the religion of the cross had power to make a believer. Christ at His weakest, His lowest, His wretchedest, struck out faith from that soldier's heart of flint. Show your world what your faith is when it is not easy to be true, when it is hard, when everything tempts one to save himself, when there is nothing but the voice of Christ saying, as He said to St. Paul, "My grace is sufficient for thee." Some one is watching you and me, silently, breathlessly, to see how firmly we can stand.

What a splendid thing it would be if when we go back to our Lord after our battle here, or our danger here, or our sorrow here, we can bring to Him a new believer won through our steadfastness; some one, a friend, a child, a servant, who first learned from us how bravely a man could live who had nothing but Christ to live for! What a triumph beyond anything that could happen to us here, if some doubting and perplexed child of God should first see the light of truth in our face, as we walked through our darkness toward Christ, the light of the world!

EASTER

1 COR. XV. 54.

Death is swallowed up in victory.

EASTER

ST. PAUL wrote his first letter to the Corinthian church to heal certain dissensions which had broken out, and also to condemn very dreadful sin which had been reported to him. It was a singular occasion to call forth the splendid words of faith and comfort with which he ends. He dealt squarely and sharply with the condition of faction and disorder and sin, and then his whole heart and mind rose above everything of the kind, and he seemed to refresh himself from the painful perplexities of this common world by looking up to the glory and the eternity of God. With a kind of a bound St. Paul seems to spring up to the truth he was so full of. Life has a meaning. It is a glorious struggle to win God. " Howbeit that is not first which is spiritual, but that which is natural; and afterward that which is spiritual. . . . Behold, I show you a mystery: We shall not all sleep, but we shall all be changed. . . . For this corruptible must put on incorruption, and this mortal must put on immortality.

So when this corruptible shall have put on incorruption, and this mortal shall have put on immortality, then shall be brought to pass the saying that is written, Death is swallowed up in victory."

The resurrection of Christ was not for St. Paul merely a hard matter which he had to accept if he would follow his Lord. The resurrection was the center of all he believed. Everything became plain by its light. If Christ did not rise, then, he said, all faith were vain. This was not the intense language of a convert, whose enthusiasm overflowed the cold and sober limits of those who had never had to fight their way into the kingdom. The whole Christian church believes its faith would be vain if it did not all happen as it is told in the matchless, simple words of the gospel. " Upon the first day of the week, very early in the morning, they came unto the sepulcher, bringing the spices which they had prepared, and certain others with them. And they found the stone rolled away from the sepulcher. And they entered in, and found not the body of the Lord Jesus. And it came to pass, as they were much perplexed thereabout, behold, two men stood by them in shining garments: and as they were afraid, and bowed their faces to the earth, they said unto them, Why seek ye the living among the dead? He is not here, but is risen. . . . And they remembered His words."

To St. Paul the resurrection was a life-and-death matter; it came to him like the answer of everything that his heart craved for. St. Paul, more than any other apostle or disciple of the Lord Jesus, seized hold of the dramatic note of Christianity. Life to St. Paul was all working out toward an end, and Christ's resurrection gave him the assurance of that end. Life was a race to run, a prize to gain, a crown to claim; and the resurrection was to St. Paul the assurance that the race would be won, that the prize would be gained, and the crown given. "Thanks be to God," he cried, "who giveth us the victory." That was what St. Paul felt he must have for his own life—victory. If he was to keep on toiling and struggling and watching and sorrowing, he must have the assurance of victory. Anything could be borne if he could have victory after. But nothing could make this life anything but vanity and folly if death crowned all.

Now when St. Paul wrote to the people of Corinth that in Christ Jesus death was swallowed up in victory, he was opening an entirely new world. The Greeks did not look at life as a progress, and they knew nothing of death as a victory. Prudence and justice and wisdom and temperance made up the ideal of the Greek. You can feel how far away that was from the energetic aims of St. Paul. Pythagoras, a Greek philosopher, is famous for saying that he was one who loved to watch the game of life. That was the height of the Greek philosophy: to be an onlooker, a cool, dispassionate, disinterested observer of other men's doings. But hear St. Paul: "I press forward, if that I may apprehend that for which also I am apprehended." To the Greek of the old days everything here in this life was final and complete and essential. To St. Paul everything here was temporary and prophetic and preparatory for something to come. To the Greek life here came to an end there; life won its triumphs here or not at all; life got its garlands now and faded out as they faded out on the grave. But to St. Paul life here was justified in life there; the shortcomings here were all made up there; all that men failed to be here, that they should be to God there. St. Paul was opening to the Greek mind a wholly new world. Greek thought, even when it is religious, is not confident or daring, but pensive and sad and wistful. A nature like that of St. Paul or St. Peter was inexplicable to the old Greeks. To the Greeks death was natural and was a part of the order of things, but to St. Paul death was unnatural and inimical and an enemy at any cost to be conquered.

It was the first-fruit of our Lord's resurrection that it transformed men's whole way of looking at death. Hitherto men looked at death as inevitable and supreme and final; after our Lord died and rose again that was all changed. The disciples of Christ were ever after fighting against death, and protesting against it, and declaring that it should be swallowed up in victory. It was sin that gave death its power. Sin kills life at the very core. Sin is always poisoning life and slackening life and deadening life, and our Lord died to take away sin. Sin and death go together, and together they cease to be. When our Lord rose again He broke the power of death, and breathed a new spirit into all life, and gave us the new assurance that we should rise with Him.

So Christ rose out of the tomb, and all the world thrilled with hope. When all was darkest, then all became clearest; when the heart was sickened with promises that had utterly failed, then it sprang up with new vigor. When Christ rose again He lifted up every human heart. We men really live by hope. When hope dies out, then everything becomes difficult and useless; and when hope comes back, flashing its light back over our whole life, then everything becomes possible and easy. If mankind lost its hope in life to come, it would be as limp as the body which had lost its spine. Some one is telling you that the belief in immortality has only a slight influence on men's conduct. The truth about it is that we men speak little about our immortality—less, brethren, than we ought to do; but we feel it more deeply and assume it more in everything we do or say than ever before. We do not consciously think much about our immortality because we are pushing forward so intensely to it. Neither does the runner consciously think much about the goal he is driving for; but if you told that runner in the midst of his race that his goal was a mere dream of his imagination, would he maintain his pace? He would sink down in a dead faint of disappointment. So would man if he discovered there was no life to come. Tell the man in the midst of his temptation that there is no final judgment or reckoning for his faithfulness; that, whether he stands firm or yields, death devours all. If the dead rise not, will it make any difference with him? If the task or the duty or the watch or the battle of this life does not have its reward and vindication in the next life, then our poor human efforts are going to be paralyzed with despair.

St. Paul did not say, death is swallowed up of life, but death is swallowed up in victory. How very profound the Bible is! What a world there is in a single word when the Holy Spirit inspires the word! It is not enough to give us life back again. We want victory; we want the life that is victorious over the grave; we want the life that has solved something, that has surmounted something. God could not satisfy a human soul by giving it merely a new chance of life and yet with all the old sins ready to drag it down again. We want victory over that sin. We cannot endure the thought of immortal life as a mere perpetual mill-round, the same pining and desire, the same struggling and straining, with the same disappointment and defeat. It is not victory if we pass through our trial and never gain any new power that makes all other trials easier to bear. Paradise itself can have no peace for the soul that has not won the victory over itself. Such a soul may pass into paradise, but it cannot be at peace until it has gotten the victory over itself. I do not want my problems solved for me; I want the power given me of solving them myself. I want all my problems swallowed up in victory. I do not want my failure merely made good to me; I want the new power by which I shall not fail again. Immortal life would be torture if it were merely a new life, but no victory, merely a rescue, merely a strength that has been thrust on me, merely a power that I had never awakened in myself. Immortal life would be immortal shame if it were merely an escape from the perplexities, the dangers, the vicissitudes, of this life, and not a new heart to conquer them. What is sadder in this world than the life that never gets any victory over its special enemy, that never is any wiser for its failure, or any stronger for its struggle, or any more patient for its trial, or any more believing for its sorrow? Nature is really mournful. Nature is the monotonous sequel of life and death—life forever swallowed up in death, and death merely stemmed for a time by life. There is never any advance in nature, or any victory. There are those who are never schooled by anything they suffer; there are those who never grow any kinder for their years, whose lives never seem to grow under their burden. Life is a mere prolongation for them, but no progress. To fail or to fall, to lose and to grieve, till time wear out the memory of these things—that is common human nature and human nature's weakness; but to fail or to fall, to lose and to grieve, and thereby gain a new depth and submission and courage, and to be ever after better able to meet any fortune or lot— that is victory.

Our Lord rose up, and then death was swallowed up in victory. His resurrection means that all the world is leavened with hope and courage. All that is in us points to victory at some time. We need not mind if there is work to do now or hardships to bear now; it shall be all swallowed up in victory. It takes a battle to bring peace. Did you ever know of any peace that did not come through fighting one's battle out? It takes sorrow to bring comfort. Did you ever know of any comfort that did not come through trusting God in sorrow? It takes doubt, too, to bring faith out into all her strength. Did you ever know of any faith that had not in some way fairly fought itself out through doubt into the full assurance of belief?

What we men want to live by is the assurance that there is victory ahead, that the tangled skein of our destiny is working out a divine order at last. Christ, who comes to us on Easter morning, breathes into us the Holy Spirit; life becomes hopeful and possible and worth while. O my brothers, you and I are undone when we lose hope. It is not death that can conquer us, for men have faced death fearlessly; but when we despair, then we are lost; when there is no outlook, nothing to press forward to, nothing to hope for, then the spirit is broken. Christ brought us not merely life, but victory. Try to think of Christ rising victorious over sin and the grave. He did not stay behind with the cross; the grave could not close around Him for good. He rose again. He tells us poor, worried, fear-haunted, burdened men and women that we too shall not stay behind with our fears and our mistakes and our cares and our griefs; we shall not stay behind with the weakness that comes to us all in time; we shall not be content with the resignation that comes to us all in time; we shall not linger along with the sorrow that comes to us all in time; no, nor with the death that comes to us all in time; but we shall rise with Christ. It is victory that is in the air to-day. Sin, darkness, and the grave have done the worst with Him who was the best, and all is over, and Christ is gone up on high. I shall yet be what I have failed to be here; I shall yet see those whom I have lost here; and there in heaven my love shall be satisfied. I shall find Him whom I have followed darkly here, and though here I have wandered from Him, lost Him, mourned for Him, seen Him afar off, run to Him, clung to Him, yet shall I at last rest in Him with the unspeakable peace that crowns my strife.

THE SECRET OF COURAGE

St. Matt. xiv. 31.

And immediately Jesus stretched forth His hand, and caught him.

THE SECRET OF COURAGE

THE day before our Lord had miraculously fed the multitude of five thousand men, with women and children. We read that after all had been filled our Lord straightway constrained His disciples to get into a ship. "And when He had sent the multitudes away, He went up into a mountain apart to pray: and when evening was come, He was there alone." Now in the fourth watch of the night, when the disciples were far out on the lake, and the water boisterous with the wind, Jesus suddenly appeared walking on the sea. But the disciples when they saw Him were troubled, and cried out for fear. But straightway Jesus said unto them, "It is I; be not afraid." And Peter, always the forward disciple, answered Him and said, "Lord, if it be Thou, bid me come unto Thee on the water." And He said, "Come." But when Peter started to go to Jesus, and saw the water swollen with the wind, he was afraid; "and beginning to sink, he cried, saying, Lord, save me. And immediately Jesus stretched forth His hand, and caught him."

Our Lord did not do His wonderful works to startle men or to gain support to Himself, but to show men that the world, and all the powers and forces of the world, were under the hand of a Master who is higher than they. The Lord of the world can do what He will with the world He has made. Jesus told His disciples that when they were filled with the Spirit of God they should do what things He did, and greater still. So it is the power of God working through men to-day that feeds the multitudes, restores the sick to life again by miraculous cures and operations, forecasts storms, flashes news in an instant around the world. These things are miraculous just as our Lord's works were miraculous; only our miracles are done by second hand, as it were, by letting the mind and power of God work freely through us, and they are done slowly and painfully. Our Lord did His miracles by His own right, and He did them instantly, and therefore they astonished men. All that we do must come from Him whose power we use. We have been taught that the achievements of our modern age come from obeying nature. Lord Bacon made this idea famous by his maxim, "Man conquers nature by obeying her." The disciple of Christ, however, knows there is something better than that. He conquers nature not by obeying nature, but by obeying nature's Lord. Obey nature—nature! Why, we obey nature just as much when we die as when we live. It is just as natural to be ignorant as to be learned, just as natural to sin as to resist evil. We obey nature just as much when we eat the poison or detect it. The laws of nature go on forever in the same blind, heedless, impersonal way. No; men have made all their progress and overcome all their dangers and learned all the secrets of life not by obeying nature, but by rising above nature to Him who is the Lord of nature. Nature has never stretched forth her hand to save man from falling; but the human heart knows One who, when He heard His disciple cry unto Him, "immediately stretched forth His hand, and caught him."

When Peter heard that wonderful command across the storm, "Come," he started, with his eye on his Lord. But then he looked down at the sea swelling at his feet, and he thought of how unheard-of a thing it was for a man to walk on the water, and he began to sink.

So it is with ourselves. We take our eyes from our Lord and we look down at the waters under us. Brethren, who is there among us who does not at times feel himself sinking, and is it not always after we have been thinking a great deal about our chances and forgetting Him who commanded us to come to Him? One has only to think of life and its risks and chances and then he cannot help trembling. There are many burdens that may prove too heavy as time goes on. There are so many on whom one must depend, and any one of whom may betray one's trust. How easily illness comes, and when one is unprepared! A dreadful accident may happen at any time, and then with what a crash comes down the structure of all one's hopes and plans!

A mother holds her little child in her arms and thinks of all the wanderings, all the disappointments, all the sorrows, all the sins, and just for a moment her eyes fill with tears and her courage is gone. How like it all is to Peter walking on the sea! But Jesus "immediately stretched forth His hand, and caught him."

We start to go to Christ, and then we begin to wonder whether we have the strength to reach Him. But the strength of a man's life does not come from his own powers. A man's strength comes from all that he forgets himself in and that is above him. It is our hopes that make us strong; it is our dreams and longings and prayers that make us strong. We are kept up by all that we trust to. When you look at the world and see how stormy life is, and how weak your own powers are, and how much there is to thwart you, then you begin to sink. You know that the man who is all the while looking out for danger does not get anywhere. The sick man who is all the while dwelling on his ailment does not get well. The writer who is always thinking about his style loses that indefinable quality of conviction that is worth all the rest put together. The leader who is always watching his influence sees it forever slipping away from him. We seem never to reach the journey's end that we are continually measuring off. Get your mind off yourself if you are ever to be well, strong, at peace, happy, comforted. Get your mind off yourself; lose yourself. Fix your eye on your Lord. A man in this world has always done his best by the utter abandonment of himself to what he loved or hoped for or believed in. It has always been through that bold rush of self-forgetfulness that men have fought their sins, won their battles, solved their problems, painted their pictures, sung their songs, scaled earth's walls, and climbed to heaven.

This is our Lord's lesson. Do not live with your eyes down on this world, but walk with your eyes fixed on your Lord. How perfectly vain it is to trust ourselves! We know no more, in truth, of how we are really held up, or of how the life of our bodies is sustained, or of how a way of escape is made just when it seemed as though everything we feared would fall upon us,—we know no more, in truth, of how the great world brings us day by day the strength to live,—than Peter knew how he walked on the water to go to Jesus. He only knew that "immediately Jesus stretched forth His hand, and caught him." That is the faith which has always made men bold. Do not think that the great soldiers of this world are the only ones who show courage. The courage of Alexander and Napoleon is pale beside that of Elijah and St. Paul. The men of this world cannot be as courageous as the men who have their eye fixed on Christ, who says, "Be of good cheer; I have overcome the world." Christ belongs so truly to a man's life that when we start to go forth we are forced, almost in spite of ourselves, to look to Him to lead. Is it not true that the men of action in the world have almost always been the believers? Something in the man who has really run in the race of life will not let him be satisfied with a world without God. Essayists and thinkers and writers have often been skeptical and denying, but the men who have led other men on the field of war, the soldiers, and the men who have sailed their ships into unknown waters, the great explorers and discoverers, these men have almost always been believing men. They have not always been devout men, I grant you; the rough trade of war or adventure has not favored that; but they have been men with a deep-rooted conviction that there was a power that led them on. The men who have opened up continents, led great armies into battle, founded nations, the men like De Soto and Champlain and Lord Lawrence and Sir John Franklin and Washington, these men, the men of action, have been believing men. They had their eye fastened on their Lord, and it made them bold.

By two qualities men accomplish most of what they are set here on earth to do. First, by their peace, and that they reach through the quiet of their lonely prayers. Our Lord, you remember, was continually going apart to pray. And then, secondly, men accomplish their fine work here in this storm-set world through their courage, and that Christ is forever pouring into the heart of every one who looks up to Him. Through peace and through courage, that is the Christian's two-edged sword; peace in the heart, and as peaceful when the world is stormiest, and courage shining out of the face. Men look at Christ, and then they cease to think of their own weakness; then they work and plan with a heart aflame, with a winning audacity. You see it by the way they spurn the earth, by the way they despise the cross, by the way they put sin and temptation under their feet. The world is dark and raging, and they are beset with trouble and sick with care, but over every other voice they hear the voice of Christ say "Come," and they are strong.

Read the books that thrill with faith and conviction. Keep your heart always near brave men. Have their pictures before you. Have their words in your mind. When you feel weak and dispirited get alongside some one who is brave with Christ. Do not satisfy every appetite of your heart, but satisfy the one highest appetite for courage. Do not strive after everything that is comfortable and nothing that is heroic. It is being filled with this world that takes away your courage; it is fixing your eye on this world that makes you sink; on this world's chances, on the praise of men, on the power of money, on rich surroundings, on the hope of influence and the dangers of life. Our Lord bids us come unto Him on the water; He bids us set faithfulness above everything else in life; He bids us train ourselves to self-denial. Surely we should not lie down at night with our last thought about our disappointments, but about the peace that Christ is leading us to. Surely we should not wake in the morning to think first of our ambitions, but first of our prayers. Stop thinking of how men have failed you, and think of Christ, who never failed a man yet; think of Christ, who never yet made a real disciple that He did not make him something of a hero besides. Whenever a man has looked up from this world and has cried, " Lord, save me," Jesus has " immediately stretched forth His hand, and caught him."

WHITSUNDAY

Acts II. 1-4.

And when the day of Pentecost was fully come, they were all with one accord in one place. And suddenly there came a sound from heaven as of a rushing mighty wind, and it filled all the house where they were sitting. . . . And they were all filled with the Holy Ghost, and began to speak with other tongues, as the Spirit gave them utterance.

WHITSUNDAY

WHEN our Lord ascended up into heaven it must have filled the disciples at first with dismay. Hitherto they had lived with their Lord and had looked to Him in every doubt or difficulty. Then, with the command to go forth and bring in the kingdom of God, He left them to themselves. There never can have been such humble means for doing such a stupendous work. The whole idea of a universal church, embracing men of different races and ways of feeling, was in itself a brand-new idea, almost an incredible idea, and those who were charged to fulfil this idea were not senators of Rome or great generals or powerful leaders, known to all the world, but twelve unlearned and simple fishermen, who had never been outside of the little province of Palestine and thought Jerusalem the wonder of the world.

That was the hard moment for the Christian church. If the disciples had the courage for their task, they had hardly any idea of how to begin, and they were almost certain to disagree and each insist on his own way. There was no longer a Lord to look to for guidance, but they were thrown on themselves, and for the moment the Christian church hung in the balance. And then a strange event occurred; for "when the day of Pentecost was fully come, they were all with one accord in one place. And suddenly there came a sound from heaven as of a rushing mighty wind, and it filled all the house where they were sitting. And there appeared unto them cloven tongues like as of fire, and it sat upon each of them. And they were all filled with the Holy Ghost, and began to speak with other tongues, as the Spirit gave them utterance. . . . Now when this was noised abroad, the multitude came together, and were confounded, because that every man heard them speak in his own language. . . . Parthians, and Medes, and Elamites, and the dwellers in Mesopotamia, and in Judea, and Cappadocia, in Pontus, and Asia, Phrygia, and Pamphylia, in Egypt, and in the parts of Libya about Cyrene, and strangers of Rome, Jews and proselytes, Cretes and Arabians," all heard from the apostles' lips the "wonderful works of God."

The apostles sat together and thought of the task that lay before them, and how impossible it was to perform, and then they thought of the Lord who had come down to earth for their sakes, till suddenly they were seized with a strange fervor and desire, and as they looked at one another a strange light seemed to hover and divide over their heads, and their hearts began to burn, and the task at which they had just now despaired they now began to yearn to do. It seemed as though a mysterious Spirit took possession of them, and illuminated them, and pointed out to each his work, and made the part that each had to do seem real and possible.

Try to understand what this miracle really was. It cannot mean that the apostles were miraculously endowed with the power to speak in a strange language, so that from their usual Aramaic speech they began to talk in the various dialects of Asia. It is not necessary to suppose anything so self-contradictory as that. Remember that Greek was a kind of universal speech in those days, and people from all those countries named could have understood the apostles if they had spoken in Greek. But what was hitherto unintelligible to all those peoples was that they could all be embraced in a common faith in a common God. In those days each country had its own national god, whose power was confined to his own country. It was unintelligible that the God whom one race worshiped and served could be worshiped and served by another. The wonderful idea that dawned in their minds was that, under all these different forms and customs, they were all worshiping the same God. When the apostles preached Christ, the incarnate Son of God, these different races, from Rome to the Euphrates, seemed to realize that it was the same Father reaching down and delivering them from sin. That was why they were all amazed. The idea of the catholic church, the universal kingdom of God, broke in on them with the force of a revelation. That was the mighty and mysterious operation of the Holy Ghost. There were no longer to be gods of Rome and gods of Greece, and a special divinity for Ephesus and for Jerusalem and for Thebes, but there was one God, who was above all and in them all, and who was no respecter of persons. It was on the day of Pentecost that there was given unto men the radiant vision of the catholic, the universal church, embracing all lands, all races, and making of one blood all nations of men for to dwell on all the face of the earth.

Do not understand me to say that Christianity first gave the world the idea of one God, who made all the world and is the Father of all mankind. That is not true. The idea had been put forth, here and there, among old writers of Greece and Rome. Christianity did not give the idea to the world for the first time, but something far more important than that. It was the Christian church that first took the idea and based human society upon it. It is not very important who first expresses a certain idea, so long as the idea is left to lie dormant. Life begins, civilization begins, when an idea is taken and is made the basis on which men are led to live together. It is always the idea at work that really counts. Christianity took the idea of human brotherhood in the one God and Father and set it at work. Cicero, who was a Roman senator and orator, wrote about the love for all mankind, but Cicero merely played with the idea; it was a mere pretty fancy. Cicero had no love for all mankind, and did not believe in his heart that it was possible. The Roman playwright Terence won a storm of applause in the theater by a line in one of his plays proclaiming universal brotherhood; but the Romans of the amphitheater sat and watched with delight the wild beasts tear their captives in pieces. Sentiments such as the Romans expressed about universal brotherhood, and such as we often hear men use to-day for effect, have a very sad sound of mockery about them. The men who say these fine things do not believe in them, and they only make it harder for those who are sincere. But when the apostles on the day of Pentecost were all of one accord in one place, and when their hearts failed them, thinking of how they should bring the gospel of Christ to all mankind, they were suddenly filled with the Holy Ghost, and they left all, and went forth, and bore persecution, and met hardship, and often gave up their lives for His sake who sent them to preach the gospel of one God, the Father. Then first of all in the history of the world was the idea of human brotherhood in God made the basis of society, and men tried to show forth in their lives what they were saying with their lips.

Now the new thing that the Christian church gave to the world was not, I say, the mere idea of human brotherhood, but the Christian church realized the idea. The Romans of the first century used to remark, "How these Christians love one another!" At the altar, where they knelt to receive the same Lord, master and slave were side by side. The Christian church told men that the tie that made them brothers of a common Father was not a figure or a fancy. She showed men how they were made one because a person had entered into them and made them one; a divine person was continually penetrating them and consolidating them. The Christian church taught that as the Father was God, so the Son was God; and how wonderful to think they, the scattered and unsophisticated and despised disciples of Christ, were bound up in the fellowship of God the Holy Ghost! I suppose there is no thought harder to put into human speech than the Godhead of the Holy Ghost. Human words seem to reel under the load of expressing this thought. It seems so elusive; it seems like merely saying over again that God the Father is ever present with us; and yet there is the plain faith of the church, which has always been strong as she has believed in God the Holy Ghost, and always been weak as she has faltered about it. The Christian church taught that the unity or brotherhood or fellowship in which all men live is a personal existence. All mankind is one, because it is the office of God the Holy Ghost to continually draw all men nearer together and make them one. She gave this wonderful new thought to mankind, that God the Holy Ghost was a divine person in the world and the hearts of men. She taught men that real unity is always the unity in a person. It is not Parliament that makes all England one, but the priceless memory of all the heroic persons who have gone into the idea of England. It is King Alfred and Richard the Lion Heart and Ridley, Latimer and Queen Elizabeth and Lord Nelson and Gordon— these make England the common object of men's passionate love. It is not the acts of Congress that make America a united people, but the common love and veneration for Washington and Warren and Franklin and Lincoln—this makes us one. It is the spirit of men of a nation that really unifies a nation. It was the memory of Washington that really broke the cause of the Rebellion. What Washington sacrificed everything for could not be wantonly destroyed. It was the spirit of Moses in the Jews that made a united people out of a horde; and the romantic love for King David kept alive the idea of the nation through disaster and exile, and burns in the Jew to-day. It takes a person to bind men together, and when our Lord ascended up into heaven He gave us God the Holy Ghost to be the Comforter, and to continually inspire us and cheer us and unite us and sanctify us, until we all should be one.

Now, brethren, it is just as possible for us as for the Romans to have fine ideas without having a particle of faith in them. Do not let the sacred thought of human brotherhood be a mere cant expression. Try to feel how true it is. Remember that God the Holy Ghost is the living tie between men. He is the everlasting proof of the oneness of mankind. He is continually discovering to each of us how we stand or fall together, how we are all of a piece, all staked on the one common welfare, and the injury to one is an injury to all. I know how possible it is to harp on human brotherhood until it seems sickly sentimentalism, and as though the idle and reckless and incompetent were to be left free to prey on those who are diligent and prudent and painstaking. But Christianity does not mean communism. Christianity means a warm, kind, and thoughtful regard for every man as a brother. It means that sense of common humanity which seems to be utterly wanting to the nations who do not accept Christ. To a Christian every man, no matter if an entire stranger, is also always something of a friend. The same Holy Spirit moves in us all and makes us brothers. Greater than anything we can make of ourselves is that which God has made us to be—the brotherhood in Christ. Nothing that divides men, their speech, their manners, their knowledge, their wealth, nothing can equal that which unites them in Christ, the Son of man. Richer than any possession is that which is given to every one—the heart of a brother. Prize all that you have in common. Be glad of the things which prove our common heritage. Every man has something in him to honor, something to revere, some innocency or courage or faithfulness. Try to find it. You remember the apostles seemed to speak to each man in the tongue in which he was born. They got down below the mere surface differences of race and dialect, and spoke the mother speech of the human heart; and how wonderfully, then, they were all inspired! Do not be satisfied with seeing men divided off into sets and parties and stations. There are still times when we can get down below all these things and become simply human. Try to speak to each man in his own tongue; see things a little more with other men's eyes; appreciate their difficulties; honor their good points; see the best in every man; have a kindly regard for all other men. Human brotherhood means something to a Christian. God the Holy Ghost is the living bond between you and every other man. You cannot be wholly strange or aloof or careless, you cannot live, once the day of Pentecost is fully come, any longer apart or disinterested, or careless of men's welfare, of men's troubles, of men's secret wounds and prayers and hopes and fears. Be human; be a part of every other man's life, his hopes and fears, his joys and pains. Oh, what does it mean that we find it so hard to care for one another, when Christ, from the realms of glory at the right hand of God, could be moved with compassion, and could come down just to cast out of poor human hearts the ugly and deadly sins! What does it mean that we are cold and unkind and abstracted and unbrotherly, but that we have not yet realized that the day of Pentecost is fully come!

"Parthians, and Medes, and Elamites, and the dwellers in Mesopotamia, and in Judea, and Cappadocia, in Pontus, and Asia," said these astonished strangers in Jerusalem, "we do hear them speak in our tongues the wonderful works of God." These men, who had been born to isolation, and nursed in their race hatred and exclusiveness, who turned from a stranger just because he was a stranger, suddenly dreamed the most wonderful of all dreams, that men were brothers and sharers of one another's destinies; and then they saw one another in a new and strange light; for cloven tongues like as of fire seemed to sit upon each one of them, and they were all filled with the Holy Ghost; and then the world with its hard lines and divisions softened and seemed hallowed, and " fear came upon every soul: and many wonders and signs were done by the apostles. . . . And they, continuing daily with one accord in the temple, and breaking bread from house to house, did eat their meat with gladness and singleness of heart, praising God, and having favor with all the people. And the Lord added to the church daily such as should be saved."

ASCENSION-DAY

Acts 1. 9.

And when He had spoken these things, while they beheld, He was taken up; and a cloud received Him out of their sight.

ASCENSION-DAY

FOR forty days after our Lord's rising from the dead He remained on earth, and was seen of the apostles, and spoke to them of the things pertaining to the kingdom of God. It seemed then to the apostles as though everything was come true and as though everything they had dreamed of was about to be realized immediately. They could not look ahead and see all the Christian centuries to be lived through, all the persecution, all the imprisonment, all the backsliding, all the weakness in times of danger, all the sin in times of prosperity, before the world could begin to look like a Christian world. They saw only Christ risen from the dead and filled with a wonderful exaltation, as though He had entered on His triumph. "When they therefore were come together, they asked of Him, saying, Lord, wilt Thou at this time restore again the kingdom to Israel?" But our Lord said unto them, "It is not for you to know the times or the seasons, which the Father hath put in His own power. But ye shall receive power, after that the Holy Ghost is come upon you: and ye shall be witnesses unto Me both in Jerusalem, and in all Judea, and in Samaria, and unto the uttermost part of the earth." They looked only for a *restored Jewish* church and nation; but Christ's kingdom was vastly wider than that, and after overflowing Jerusalem and filling all Judea, it then penetrated into Samaria, with whom the Jews, as you remember, had no dealings, for the Samaritans were a mixed people, and finally it broke out free from all Jewish influence and constraint, and His disciples have been witnesses of Him unto the uttermost parts of the earth.

Forty days after His resurrection Christ ascended up into heaven. He had showed Himself alive after His passion by many infallible proofs, being seen of them forty days, and teaching them what His will was in regard to the new kingdom. Our Lord did not leave it to His apostles to create just what kind of a church they saw fit; our Lord gave to the apostles commandments which they were to obey. The Bible says so. He did not merely stop on the margin of this earth for a moment to give them a general commandment, "Preach and baptize," but for forty days our Lord was seen by the apostles, and for forty days He spoke to them of the things pertaining to the kingdom of God. Then, when all was done and He had left them equipped for all that was to come, when He had provided—oh, the wonder of it!—for all the perils and pitfalls that lay in wait for the church, provided for all the weakness and sin and pride and folly of His own followers, and had foreseen and forestalled it all with express provision, then, " when He had spoken these things, while they beheld, He was taken up; and a cloud received Him out of their sight." Right out of their midst, while the earth trembled and the earth shook, the Lord arose. A mysterious distance seemed to grow between them,—the disciples and the Lord,—and they saw Him disappear as a cloud received Him out of their sight. Our Lord vanished not because He went away, but because He took again His divine perfection, and transcended thereby the power of mortal eyes to see Him. When He ascended up into heaven He did not really go away. Of course up and down, ascending and descending, are mere figures in such a world as ours. Heaven is no more up than it is down; it is a higher order of being. When our Lord was born on earth He stooped down in the scale of spiritual life and became visible to mortal eyes, and when His work was done and His sacrifice once offered He rose again and resumed once more the spiritual perfection in which He became to them invisible. The Bible does not say He went away, but He was taken up; a cloud received Him out of their sight. It is only a spiritual being that can bow itself and come down, and can then rise again. It is only a spiritual being that can unbend, and can forego its powers, and be content for a time to be less than itself and live on a lower plane to reveal itself. But when it resumes its true nature and perfection it does not go away; it simply transcends the power of those who live in the lower plane to see. When our Lord's work was done He rose again, "and a cloud received Him out of their sight."

There are two worlds, brethren, in which we live, the one as real as the other, although the one is visible and the other is invisible. Our bodies belong to the visible world, but our souls belong to the world of spirits. Our Lord passed at will from one to the other. He came down, and was made man, and was visible to men, and then He rose, and resumed His divine nature, and became invisible. When we die our bodies decay, but our souls live on and, free of the body, belong wholly to the world of spirits. Our souls do not go away at death, but they enter a higher order of being. That which restrains them and clogs them and obstructs them is done away. Just what kind of life the life after death is no one knows; but the reason why we do not know is not because God does not want us to know, or denies us the light we crave to have, but because our mortal eyes cannot see into the spiritual world. Those whom we mourn as dead are not really gone away, but a cloud has received them out of our sight. The world of spirits is as near to us now as it will be after death; but we are blind, we are earthly, we are not innocent enough or chastened enough or purified enough, and therefore we cannot see.

But the church gives us Ascension-day in which to concentrate our minds on the world of spirits. Immortal life is not left by our church to take its chance among all the thoughts that press on men's minds; a day is set for us to dwell on it. We see our Lord rising from earth and heaven closing around Him. He is in that world of spirits, not gone away, but only hidden from sight. All that we most want to know the church lets us see with our own eyes. We do not speculate whether the dead live again, but we see our Lord rise out of our sight and enter paradise. To merely speculate about future life seems a terrible trifling with human hearts. Those who feel their hearts bound up now as much as ever with the hearts of those who are entered into rest cannot argue about immortality. That is a frightful insult to a heart that bleeds at the thought of what it has lost. No, brethren, the church does not argue. When we ask bread of her she does not give us a stone, or when we ask an egg she will not offer us a scorpion. To those who are hungry to know whether they shall see their dead again, she has no controversy, no syllogisms, no hair-drawn arguments, no fine-spun probabilities. She points to her Lord, who, " while they beheld, was taken up; and a cloud received Him out of their sight." Oh, do you not feel the comfort and assurance of it? What kind of a heart can a man have who can debate coolly whether the one wild hunger of his soul is a dream or a reality? It is not the church who trifles so with the human heart, but she calls men to look and see for themselves. Christianity is based on facts—not doctrines, but facts. The church always deals with the facts; the church never argues or speculates or balances evidences or probabilities. The church points to her Lord with one world fading away from Him and another receiving Him into the cloud of its perfection. Men may debate about these sacred mysteries, men who have cast off religion; men who have outgrown the incarnate Son of God may speculate about a future life and leave us with their flimsy guesses; but the church never. The church is always concrete, plain, direct, real, satisfying. She never guesses; she is never abstract or far-fetched. She does not reason about immortality, as Socrates did while he fondled his chains for the last time on earth, but she shows her Lord; she gives us Ascension-tide. She falls on her knees and prays, and lo, " while they beheld, He was taken up; and a cloud received Him out of their sight." She lifts the veil, and there is the world of eternity palpitating behind all that we see or do. There are those whom we love; there are those whom to see again makes all of some men's hope in life; those whom we mourn; those whom we misjudged here; those whom to see but for a moment, and to fall down before and claim whose forgiveness, would be like cold water on the tongue of him who is tortured with thirst. They are there behind that cloud, which simply marks the limit of our sight.

That is your church which celebrates in these seasons of the Christian year not theories or pious fancies, but she celebrates at Christmas and Easter and Ascension-day the great facts of the spiritual world. Here is the church's altar, where the blessed drama of immortality is revealed plain before your eyes. Men's hearts here on earth are failing them for fear; their eyes are blind with the smoke and dust of this troubled world. In this world all is dark and uncertain and clouded, but there, through the visible signs of bread and wine,—there is Christ, breathing peace and hope and cheer into human hearts. Christ stands in the world of spirits and shows Himself to us. He does not stand alone, but those who have found Him, though lost to us, they are there too, suddenly, mystically, but really present to our spiritual eyes.

It is not strange that death seems a very mournful subject to those who persistently put it away from them. It does not seem mournful to one who looks at death in the light of our Lord's ascension, and who knows that beyond that cloud of our earthly blindness there is Christ still. To such a believer it seems not the most dreadful thing, but the most sublime thing, that we are to pass to a life of which eye hath not seen, nor ear heard, the things which God hath prepared for those that love Him. How blind we are content to be to all the real meaning of our life or of our loves! How strange that we should lose the real purpose of life in the mere multitude of the cares of living! How like jewels on a shining cord are strung all the significant moments of a soul's history from birth to the grave, all gleaming with the light of our Lord's ascension! There is the mystery of birth and of growth and of young intelligence, friendship and love, loss and gain, suffering and sickness, plenty and want, life and death. What transcendent mysteries! but we have no time to think about them. Remember Mary, who "kept all these things, and pondered them in her heart." It seems so unworthy of a child of God to go toward these experiences and crises of life, to which we are all inevitably led, with hardly ever bestowing a thought upon them. Some day pain will take a man by the hand and claim him, but he has never given a thought to God's discipline of pain. Some day he will lose his friend, his child, his life, and then there will be everything to learn about that cloud into which they have been received. Some day God will call you and me and bid us lay down all and go to Him. How untrue it is, how unfilial, how unmanly, how ashamed we shall be, how bowed with humiliation, to go before our Father and meet Him there at the throne of righteousness, a son, but a stranger, an immortal soul, but bound up in the things of this life, a man in the things of this earth, though a child in the knowledge of the things of God!

This is a most beautiful world; this is not a vale of tears. This is a beautiful world, but it is not anything in nature that makes this world seem really lovely; this is a most beautiful world because everywhere there are men and women who are faithful under a hard trust, forbearing and patient under great provocation, living as though they were alive to their great destiny.

There is nothing this world can do for us like fitting us to appear before God. St. John said, "I saw, and bare record that this is the Son of God." What a triumph that is for any life! what a glory! Not that one has never suffered or lost or despaired or sinned, but that, through suffering and loss and despair and sin, a man has found his Christ. The burden may be heavy and the problem of a man's life very hard to solve, but if in this life we can only learn that it is Christ who sent the burden and gave the problem, that throws a wonderful light on a man's path. Feel that. Find Him. That is the real end of living, to find our Lord. Every one cannot be fortunate, but every one can be faithful; every one can use his life as a discipline till, through simplicity and innocency and faith, his eyes are opened and the paradise of God is plainly revealed.

MIRACLES

St. Luke vii. 15.

And he that was dead sat up, and began to speak. And He delivered him to his mother.

MIRACLES

WE read that on a certain day our Lord entered a city that was called Nain. It was really only a little village, but it was henceforth to become known all over the world. As our Lord drew near to the gate of the city, a dead man was being carried out, the only son of his mother, and she a widow. So deep was the sympathy felt for her that a great part of the people of the village went with her to the burial. When Jesus saw her He was so moved with compassion that He came and touched the bier, while they that bore it stood still. Then He said, "Young man, I say unto thee, Arise." And he that was dead sat up, and He delivered him to his mother.

It was one simple act in the life of our Lord as He went about doing good. His life was one long labor of love. Here it was a mother who received back her only son, and she a widow; there it was a blind man who received his sight; there a forgiving word spoken, there a long infirmity healed. When you look at our Lord's life as a whole, you are struck at the succession of acts of kindness and words of sympathy and guidance. He moved among men, crowded around by the helpless and the sick and the sorrowing, always healing wounds, always removing some infirmity, always closing up the gaps which sin and misfortune and death had made.

A marvelous office it was that our Lord came to fulfil. He came to bring peace out of the struggle, and health out of sickness, and light out of darkness, and faith out of doubt, and life out of death. We can imagine how His heart rejoiced in His mission of reconciliation. It makes you very happy to do an act of kindness by which some life starts up with new courage. You feel a certain deep thrill of satisfaction when you use your fuller knowledge to help your child in his difficulties with his books; you give a boy a word out of your riper experience to save him from mistake, you come between a little child and its orphan loneliness, between a destitute family and the hunger of the children, you come in between your friend and his discouragement, and it seems so rich and precious then to be able to be of service. The greatest joy is to help another make more of his life, to open a door of opportunity to another. The very sweetest use of one's manhood, of one's experience, of one's talent, of one's means, is to bring the lives of others forward in some way, and in some way to enlarge the opportunity of men.

But if we feel such a deep joy in our poor efforts to be kind and useful to others, what must it have been for our Lord, who came with His compassion multiplied by His power? So much you want to do you do not see your way to do, so much you crave to do that you simply are not able to do; but Jesus came alone, of all mankind, with a power that was equal to His compassion. When He came down from heaven to redeem the world this deep joy must have filled His heart. He came with full power to bind up all the wounds, to stay all the hunger, to forgive all the sins, to comfort all the sorrowing, to restore all the dead. It was His blessed work to bring back hope into the hearts from which hope had long since fled, to smooth out all the lines of trouble in human faces, to start the sinful up to lead new lives. He gave back to Jairus, the ruler of the synagogue, his only daughter, and to the nobleman his only son; He cured that woman's long-standing infirmity; He sent the ten lepers away cleansed. That is our Lord, coming down to earth, and reaching with one hand to the afflicted soul, and with the other to the lost object of its love and yearning, and bringing them together to make them one.

Perhaps there is some one here who would like to answer me and say, "Yes, that is a fine way of looking at Christ's miracles, but I cannot believe that the miracles ever happened." Now is there not some one with this on his lips to say: that the laws of nature are sacred, and not even Christ could break them to bring back a dead man to life again? Brethren, I shall not think it the least strange if some one makes that reply. In fact, it is one of the commonest difficulties that we meet with, that we find people who accept all the teaching without any of the facts of Christianity. They love our Lord's deeds, but they reject His claims. They believe in all of His words and in none of His miracles. Now it would be easy to show that these things cannot be separated, and it is well to remember that it is only the church that believes in her Lord's miracles that keeps alive also the memory of His goodness and His love. But leave all this. I ask every one who has the least difficulty in believing in our Lord's miracles, because they seem to interrupt the laws of nature, to see what it really was our Lord did at the gate of the city of Nain, when he that was dead sat up, and He delivered him to his mother.

It was not our Lord who interrupted nature's laws when He did that miracle of love and healing. When our Lord gave back that only son to his mother, He was not breaking nature asunder; He was bringing together things that had been riven apart. It was sin and death that had broken nature's laws, and it was our Lord who healed the awful wound in that mother's heart. It was not natural for that young man to die; there was some lamentable ignorance, some deadly defect of constitution, there was some rank contagion that had sowed poison in the system, and therefore the lad died. Our Lord was not the interloper, the violator, of nature. Our Lord was the vindicator, the redeemer, of nature and her laws. Sin and death had broken that woman's heart. That boy belonged to his mother, and she a widow. God Almighty made them one for time and eternity, and it was death—death made that fearful havoc in her house. Do you see what I mean? Death, not our Lord, broke nature's laws. It was Christ who restored them. It was the frightful break-up of all that seemed sweet and comforting in that woman's life that moved our Lord to such compassion. It was so tragic, so sad, so devastating; the stricken mother, the large and hushed company, the air of calamity that pervaded everywhere. Love had been slain; motherhood was stabbed; the only prop of a woman's life had been wrenched away. It was all so unnatural, so hateful, so irrevocable; it was such a lie given to all that life promised to be down there in the dawn of its strength; and then the Lord Jesus Christ rose and vindicated life, love, nature, and the will of almighty God, and delivered him to his mother.

Here is a man who cannot believe in Christ's miracles because they seem to him blots on nature's uniformity; but we believe that sickness and loss and infirmity and blindness and madness and death are the terrible blots on nature's uniformity, and that our Lord, in healing the sick and casting out devils and raising the dead to life, is restoring nature. It was a black blot on a world of love and gladness when the beloved servant of the centurion was at the point to die, and when the five thousand men and women were faint for food because forgetting everything but their hunger for truth, they followed the Lord of truth into the wilderness. It was a dark blot on a world of light when the blind man cried from the wayside to receive his sight, and when the legion of devils in a man's soul had driven him away to live among the tombs. It was cruel and wrong that the fishermen should have toiled all the night and have taken nothing. It was horrible that the waves of the sea were about to ingulf the apostles who were chosen to bring deliverance to the whole world. Is all this what you call nature? Yes, but nature sick, nature lawless, nature raging, nature dumb, nature dying; but our Lord came swift from heaven to brand the enemy that had done it all—sin. Sin is the cause of all the disorder and the divisions and the calamities and the wounds of nature. It is natural to be happy and to be strong. Joy is natural, and love is natural, and success is natural, and everlasting life is natural, but there comes in sin, working like a dark distemper, and destroys it all. It is sin that works in men's hearts and makes them hate and hinder instead of loving and helping one another. It is sin that breaks down courage and destroys men through folly. There it is, that dread disease of sin at the very root of our life, and it casts its blight on everything that seemed fair and good and hopeful. But our Lord stands there, forever by His love loosing men from the bond of sin. He stands there, forever making good the losses that sin has made, repairing the breaches in life, binding up the wounds, saving those who are lost, and giving back the dead.

If you could only see Christ as He really is, your champion, your deliverer from the only real enemy that besets your life, you would feel how impossible it is for a man to live without his Lord. Sin is so dreadful. Sin is so dreadful because it is so subtle and deceiving. Sin is so dreadful because it eats away human life and works with a swift certainty of death. Everything sin does is to divide men and to destroy hopes and to break down strength, to weaken a man's courage and balk him of his hopes. But everything Christ does is to vindicate our lives, to kill out the sin that is killing us, to destroy the death that is destroying us, to put new power into us, to show men how truly the Father hath put all things into our hands, to teach us we are not born to die, that our loves here are not to come to an end. It is an enemy that makes the misery that is in the world, and that enemy our Lord came down from heaven to fight, and to free us from, until at last he shall be cast out.

Christ yearns over your life and my life. He yearns to make us understand how He is forever fighting for us. We have not the time to think much about Him, because we are struggling so hard to get certain things we want. But Christ knows that our deepest need in any trouble or loss or grief is to be free from sin. Sin makes us blind to the arm of God that all the time holds us up. Sin keeps us from knowing that Christ is the eternal witness that every wrong shall be made right, and be made right to you who have suffered; that every loss shall be made good, and be made good to you who have endured the loss; every tear shall be wiped away; every sin shall be forgiven; every doubt shall be solved; every enemy shall be subdued. With Christ here, it becomes so easy to wait and to bear and to trust. There is just one thing we need to know. Our Lord is master on this field of battle. He stands to-day as He stood in the midst of that scene of desolation, and he that was dead sat up, and He delivered him to his mother. When we know that, the veil of this earth seems to part and there is heaven. It is the land where the lost are found, where wrongs are righted, where the cruelties of this world are reversed, where the dumb speak, where the blind see, where the dead are raised, and where the pure in heart after the long toil of this life shall see God. There they who have hungered and thirsted for righteousness here, and in spite of all never doubted or turned back, shall at the last be filled.

TRINITY-SUNDAY

St. John III. 16.

For God so loved the world, that He gave His only begotten Son, that whosoever believeth in Him should not perish, but have everlasting life.

TRINITY-SUNDAY

NICODEMUS, to whom these wonderful words of our Lord were said, was a devout man, waiting, like Simeon, for the consolation of Israel. He had the trust, so common among the Jews of his day, that God would at some time show His power and destroy their enemies and restore Israel. When Nicodemus heard what things Jesus had done, he wondered whether it were not He who would do this very thing, and so, being an earnest Jew, he went to Him by night and said, "Rabbi, we know that Thou art a teacher come from God: for no man can do these miracles that Thou doest, except God be with him." But our Lord, when He saw Nicodemus, knew that his whole conception of God and God's way of working must be changed. Christ Jesus did not come to show the power of God; He came to show the love, the compassion, the sacrifice, of God; He came to make known His Father by revealing the sacrifice of the Son.

So our Lord said to him, "Thou must be born again," and Nicodemus, who suddenly felt himself standing on the threshold of a new world, said, "How can these things be?" Then our Lord said, "As Moses lifted up the serpent in the wilderness, even so must the Son of man be lifted up. For God so loved the world, that He gave His only begotten Son, that whosoever believeth in Him should not perish, but have everlasting life."

It is not hard to suppose that Nicodemus felt all his life after a great joy that the Lord had first spoken to him this charter of a new kingdom; that not power, but love, was the secret of the new life. So too it must have been a joy all her life for the Samaritan woman, that she had from the lips of her Lord His wonderful word of moral and religious freedom: "God is a Spirit: and they that worship Him must worship Him in spirit and in truth." To Martha it must always have been precious that the Lord had said to her the words, "I am the resurrection, and the life: he that believeth in Me, though he were dead, yet shall he live: and whosoever liveth and believeth in Me shall never die." Peter certainly to his dying day, and even when most overwhelmed at the thought of how he had denied the Lord, could never have ceased to thrill at the words which the Lord had spoken to him; yes, the incarnate Son had stopped and, singling out Peter, while knowing all his impatience and headstrong will, and his weakness under sudden alarms, and his habit of cooling in the face of opposition, had said to him the words, that must have felt to him like a cool hand on a hot brow, "Thou art Peter, a rock." It must be a wonderful privilege that God grants some men: to lead great armies, or to rear vast cathedrals, or sit on thrones, or sail first to a new continent, or to write a book that lives; but greater distinction than this is it that some word of universal succor and courage and peace was first spoken by the Son of man to Martha and to Peter and to John and to Nicodemus.

There is expressed in this text the thought that especially belongs to to-day. We try on Trinity-Sunday to give some account to ourselves of the great doctrine that lies at the root of all we believe; but we ought never to forget that it is the fact of the Trinity, and not the doctrine, that we are most concerned about. The Trinity is our human attempt to define the fact that God, the Creator of heaven and earth, is not a being of authority and power only, but is a person that loves and guards and guides us, His children, and no matter what dangers may befall us, holds us safely in His everlasting arms. Now it is often urged that the belief in the Trinity is not necessary to Christianity, because the word "Trinity" never occurs once in the whole Bible; but the fact of the Trinity is on every page of the Bible, although the word itself is not used once. Abstract statements of doctrine are not in the Bible at all. The Bible is a book of facts and records and histories. There is not one definite statement of an abstract doctrine in the whole Bible, but the facts out of which all the doctrines spring are there. The Bible brings out into sharp light the everlasting facts, and the doctrines grow spontaneously out of the facts.

The doctrine of the Trinity expresses the two facts of the nature of God that are equally true and yet are very hard to reconcile. On the one hand, God is a being of infinite power and awful majesty, and, on the other hand, He is a being of infinite tenderness and love. He is as mighty as He is loving, and He is as unapproachably glorious as He is gracious and full of compassion. The real problem of religious thought is to reconcile God's almighty power with God's boundless love, and it is only in the faith in the incarnate Son that they are reconciled. All men everywhere, in all times and countries and in all conditions of culture, have had some sort of belief in the God of power and might. But it is only Christianity that shows the love that is behind the power, and therefore Christianity, of all the religions, is the freest from superstition. Superstition is a state of mind where the belief in the power of God has so overshadowed the belief in the love of God that men's hearts are filled with fear and they cower down before the phantoms of their imaginations. Mere general enlightenment, then, is not enough to kill the superstition of an age. In fact, some of the ages in the world's history when general enlightenment has been greatest, like the age of Augustus and the period of the French Revolution in France, have been times when the mass of the people were sunk the lowest in superstition. The very science which we suppose dispels all trace of superstition may be the most direct cause of it, because science in revealing so many astounding things and opening up such unimagined stretches of time and space is really all the time giving us a more awful and terrifying knowledge of God. Science is adding to the burden that the mind feels already insupportable. The vaster the world becomes, the more stars of infinite distance men discover, the more secret chemical and electrical forces they detect working unseen before us, while at the same time men are no nearer to the knowledge of the incarnate Son who makes known the love that beats through and animates the power, why, then, so much the more frightful life becomes and so much the more men are tempted to hide behind superstition from the God whose awful and accusing voice they hear. Now it needs something more than enlarged knowledge to kill superstition. It needs a wholly new idea of God, such as no human discovery can give. It is Christ Jesus who lifts the weight of fear from our minds. Not science, but Christianity, not enlightenment, but the belief in the Trinity, is the real enemy of superstition. Christ Jesus came down from heaven to show us God the Father. God the Father comes first in the Christian's creed, and after that the Maker of heaven and earth. The real greatness of God is not in His power or omnipresence or eternity; the most wonderful thing about the nature of God is His love. So Christ Jesus taught us. God is love; and His love is not a mere trait, a mere element of the divine nature, one mood among many, a sunshine that streams now and then through the clouds of omnipotence, but the very nature of God is to love. He is God the Father, and His heart is forever pouring out in love to God the Son. The divine thing about God is not that He made heaven and earth, that He is here and everywhere, that He can hold the hills in the hollow of His hand, that "Thou, Lord, in the beginning hast laid the foundation of the earth; and the heavens are the works of Thine hands," and that "they shall perish, but Thou remainest," and that "they all shall wax old as doth a garment; and as a vesture shalt Thou fold them up, and they shall be changed: but Thou art the same, and Thy years shall not fail." The really divine thing about God is His love. Christ came and gave expression to all that the prophets had tried to speak with stammering lips. All that Abraham had ventured forth into a strange country to prove, all that David had sung out of his stricken heart, all that Isaiah had yearned for and strained after, all that holy men and women in Jerusalem had watched for and felt was near at hand, broke out into speech at last, when our Lord said to Nicodemus, "For God so loved the world, that He gave His only begotten Son, that whosoever believeth in Him should not perish, but have everlasting life."

The great secret of the world is that this world is ruled by almighty love. That is the great fact of which the doctrine of the Trinity is only the abstract expression; that is the great fact which men are doubting when they doubt the doctrine of the Trinity; that is the great fact that the Bible puts for us beyond all question, not by naming the doctrine, but by telling us the story of the Christ who came down from heaven that we might have life.

Love is the very nature of God. The love of God is not a mere indulgent fondness, but God loves us with that love that must give itself to us to make us like Himself. Real love can only be shown by sacrifice, and God the Father gave His only begotten Son to show His love. It is by what we bear for others that we show love. It is by all that you dare, all that you submit to, all the shame you share, all the sacrifices you make, that you show love. It is not the love you speak, but the sacrifice you show, the life you give, that makes you known. It was so that God the Father showed His love. He did not send a prophet to announce His love; He did not write it on the sky in letters of gold; He did not leave it as a divine guess; but He sent His Son to suffer and to die, that He might make known that love. It does not matter how hard it may be for you with your peculiar lot to understand that God loves you in your world. You know that He loves you, not because you can understand it, but because He gave His only begotten Son. It seemed a degrading idea to the old Romans, and they used to taunt the early Christians that their Lord and their Saviour was a crucified man, but then the only idea of God the Romans had was a God of power.

A crucified Saviour seems so incomprehensible to those who think only of God's omnipotence. For the Son of God to be born of a Jewish woman, to choose from all the kingdoms of this world the smallest, and from all the worlds of space this one world, perhaps the humblest, and to be unknown, and then despised, and to suffer and to die, this is simply incomprehensible alike to the most ignorant savage and the most learned unbeliever; for both look only for a God who manifests Himself through power. But the heart of man that has felt, that has failed, that has lost, that has yearned for peace, that has seen Christ die, although this was He that should have redeemed Israel,—that heart of man knows its Lord. What is it that speaks to the soul like that cross on which God gave His Son to save the world and show His love? He who made all loves all, and forever and forever there is God in the person of the Son with His divine arms nailed to the cross, wide opened to all the sorrows, all the loneliness, all the pains, all the despair, of men. O brethren, that is our God, the God of the cross. God, whose love can never be shut away, so loves us men with the love of a Father "that He gave His only begotten Son, that whosoever believeth in Him should not perish, but have everlasting life." Brethren, I do not ask you to accept any mystery or abstruse doctrine. I ask you to believe the most practical and most vital truth that any child of earth can conceive of, that a human soul is so precious to almighty God that all the wealth of created things is not too much to pay to save it and arouse it. Will you not believe with me in a God who, though He made the heavens and all that they contain, yet thought more of the souls of men, and because of His love for the human soul He gave everything, spared nothing, and sent even His only begotten Son to tell men of the Father? The mind of man cannot conceive anything more wonderful than that. He who is the all-powerful, all-wise, is also the all-loving. How foolish it seems to those who have seen only the vast vision of a God infinite and eternal and transcending man's power ever to think of Him aright! How foolish the God of the cross seems to them, but oh, how divine to us, how adorable to us! How easy it is for us not merely to know God, but to trust Him! How easy it is for us not merely to believe that He is, but to look up into His face and stop the secret sin that makes Him bleed afresh! How easy it is in this dark and devious world to hear His voice and then forever after stand at our post like men who have forgotten what fear was! Do not refuse that God who has been revealed by the light of all the discovery of these latter days, but do not be satisfied with it—do not be satisfied with a God who is merely incomprehensible. After you see such a divine life dawn on your heart, then go and see Him die on the cross,— there is the wonder and truth in that He died for sin once,—and know how unspeakably more precious and more real is the God who " so loved the world, that He gave His only begotten Son, that whosoever believeth in Him should not perish, but have everlasting life."

A FIXED HEART

Ps. LVII. 7.

My heart is fixed, O God, my heart is fixed.

A FIXED HEART

DAVID wrote the psalm from which this text was taken under circumstances of great peril. He was fleeing from King Saul with a price set on his head. Everywhere he saw danger and in every face a foe. The psalm is in two parts, like a poem of two stanzas. In the first he paints his despair and the horror of his foes, and then in the other he turns and cries just as passionately, "My heart is fixed, O God, my heart is fixed;" and then he forgot the snares and the venomous looks of his enemies in the joy of his trust. "Awake, lute and harp: I myself will awake right early."

But the men who wrote the psalms were not thinking of themselves only; they felt themselves the mouthpiece of the nation. These men, although they wrote out of their needs and their dangers, yet felt as patriots and gave voice to the pangs of an oppressed people. They lost themselves in a nation's danger, in the ruin of their land, in the prostration of their faith. It gives any man who speaks or writes or leads a sense of exaltation as his own personal fears and perils and sorrows are transfigured into the fears and the perils and the sorrows of the multitude. Strangely enough, the very act of rising above a man's own interests and seeing the danger on that larger scale brings peace and security and confidence. When David felt himself caught in the large, deep current of his country's destiny, then his confidence returned and he could say, " My heart is fixed, O God, my heart is fixed."

There are many who doubt whether it is possible for a man to-day to say, " My heart is fixed, O God, my heart is fixed." There are so many ideas that have changed in only a generation, there are so many views that have broadened, and there are so many beliefs that have been entirely given up, that it seems impossible any more for a man's heart to be fixed. It seems like deliberately shutting the eyes and stopping the ears to hope that the change is all over and that from now on there will never be anything discovered or thought out to reverse our judgments. Men are coming forward to-day with the startling assertion that no one can say with certainty that he will believe to-morrow what he believes to-day. A new discovery or a new excavation may in one night, it is feared, upset the best-established convictions. There are few men to-day who believe that the world is only six thousand years old, although not so long ago that was scarcely questioned. When we were children we were taught that the interior of the earth was a ball of molten fire and the outside was a mere crust, but that view is hardly held now. Men used to take the inspiration of the Bible to mean that the identical words of the Hebrew and the Greek were dictated by the Holy Spirit, but men see now that on the face of it that is impossible. Men once held that Christianity was the only sincere religion, and that Mohammed and Gautama and Confucius were conscious impostors. A man would be ashamed to acknowledge such a belief now. Men once believed that all unbaptized infants were damned eternally. Certainly the heart of man is not fixed on that.

There are many things that cannot be fixed. A man's views about the dates and composition of the books of the Bible cannot be fixed; a man's views about the ritual or the government of the church cannot be wholly fixed; a man's views about the nature of God's just retribution, or the nature of the life to come, cannot be fixed. Nothing final about these matters has been granted to men either in the Bible or the creeds. Almighty God trusts men, under the guidance of the Holy Spirit, to press on ever toward such truth, although we may never reach it here on earth.

But it was something very different that the psalmist meant when he sang that song of Israel, "My heart is fixed." It was no view about the law or the Jewish ceremonial that fixed Israel's heart as she went out to battle with Assyria, and was worsted, and was driven away into exile. That fixed heart of Israel had something that no defeat or conquest or exile could disturb, and that was an indestructible faith that, in spite of everything that happened, she was under the sure guidance of God. It was not the mind of Israel, the philosophy of Israel, the ritual of Israel, the government of Israel, that was fixed. It was the heart, the heart that loved and prayed and waited and trusted: "My heart is fixed, O God, my heart is fixed."

We find in men two tendencies: one is to hold on to everything, and the other to hold on to nothing. To the one everything is equally sacred, and to the other it is equally a matter of dispute. No amount of proof will loosen the one man's hold, while to the other the telescope or the laboratory may in a night destroy everything he held sure. The one man lacks outreach, and the other man lacks rooting, but neither one has any fixed heart.

A Christian's heart is fixed on that which is almost as old as the hills. The essence of your faith, the solid core of it, Abraham had almost four thousand years ago. Our faith in God is Abraham's faith, only fuller and lighted up with all the glory that shone from the face of Jesus Christ. It is stronger and surer for every heart that has been fixed by it since Abraham. Has it not worn well, this faith of ours? It has lived on through the downfall of five great universal kingdoms, Assyria, Babylon, Persia, Greece, and Rome. It went down to Egypt with Jacob; it went forth to Canaan with Moses. It battled with the heathen. It rose in triumph under David; it sank back under defeat and destruction. It rebuilt its Holy City. It waited for Christ; it founded the church and charged the apostles. It worked in the mines; it died at the stake; it endured persecution and loss. It fought the barbarians and converted them. It saved Europe. It kept strong when men were ignorant and debased. It quickened with the Renaissance; it purified itself in the Reformation. It fainted during the eighteenth century; it rallied again and rode the storm of the French Revolution. It burst out again in this century in splendid missionary zeal. It is to-day stronger, broader, surer than it ever was before. It springs to the Christian's lips to-day with the courage of four thousand years of battle and humiliation and wasting and watching and triumph. It is all the history of God's succor from the time of Abraham that goes into a man's words when he says to-day, "My heart is fixed."

Times there have been, indeed, brethren, when the outlook was dark. It was dark when Israel lay in bondage in Egypt. It was very dark when the chosen people were scattered by Nebuchadnezzar. It was terribly dark when our Lord hung on the cross, and all the disciples forsook Him and fled. It was dark in the middle ages, when the church lay dormant and sinful and corrupt, and when the prince of this world seemed to sit on the very throne of God. I do not wonder that there were unbelievers in the fourteenth and fifteenth centuries, when a pope's word would not be believed under oath. I do not wonder there were unbelievers when the dazzling light of the New Learning came in on the darkened understanding of those times, or in the age of the French Revolution, when a wave of doubt swept Europe, and when science seemed so new and strong, and religion so old and weak. I do not wonder that the faith of men faltered. But I do wonder that in this day, after so many struggles and trials and tests, after the faith has survived so much, endured so much, suffered so much, triumphed over so much, I wonder that, looking back along that line of light that threads the years of cloud and darkness, there is one of us who does not say with all the effort of his soul, "*My* heart is fixed, O God, *my* heart is fixed."

Do not be afraid to say that; do not apologize for it. The greatest thing about a man is the fixedness of his heart. When men say they cannot be sure of believing to-morrow what they believe to-day, they do not know of what kind of eternal stuff a man's soul is made. The very essence of belief is that it is something never to be changed, fixed and eternal. If there is no eternal belief there is no belief at all. Belief means that, no matter what may happen, it will stand fast; belief is the insight of an eternal soul looking beyond time and chance. The man who has not come to believe in something that will last on to all eternity has not yet found out what there is down deep in his soul. It is only a man who is born for eternity who can be brought as a child to baptism, and can promise through its sponsors what it will afterward adopt in its own name and what every year of its life will only strengthen and confirm.

You cannot indeed tie up the mind of man, for the mind expands with new light; but the growth of a soul lies in the fixedness of its trust, its love, its loyalty. It is the very nature of a mind that it is something that expands, and it is the very nature of a heart that it is something that is fixed. You cannot build on a foundation that does not remain the same; you cannot develop what does not preserve its identity. The faith in Christ has broadened and deepened, but it has remained, in truth, the same as on the first day. Do you suppose that, if St. Augustine came back to earth, he would not find in Christ to-day all that he stood for and staked his life on? Do you suppose that, when fifteen hundred years more are passed by, that same faith will not be held? Could we in fifteen hundred years from now come back to earth again, we should not recognize its science or its inventions, the organization of society, the means of transportation. I doubt not men will ride through the air then as they ride on the land now, that travel will be of a marvelous velocity, that Africa will be settled like Europe, that the north pole will have been reached; but I also doubt not that men will rise to sing the Te Deum and to say the Apostles' Creed, and that the same Bible will be venerated, and the same church loved, the same altar bear the same bread that cometh down from heaven, the same Christ who is above all and in you all.

The best thing there is about us men and women is our loyalty, our power of standing fast, of pledging our soul for time and eternity. Because we are eternal souls, we cannot help believing eternally. We want loyalty and the willingness to wait. When we meet with a doubt or a difficulty we ought to wait until Christ speaks. Shame on us if the reading of a single book, or a single argument of an unbeliever, can divert the stream of the faith of four thousand years from flowing through us and refreshing us. There are working-men criticizing the church to-day, although since the time of Abraham there has not been a century when the church did not take a brave stand for the poor. There are men and women to-day doubting God because of their misfortunes or their sufferings, although from the dawn of history men have transformed their lives and glorified humanity through their trust. Read all the books you like, but remember that Christian faith is not an argument, but it is an affair of loyalty. Your mind ought to receive new impressions, but your heart ought to be fixed. God Almighty made you a child of His, and to all eternity nothing can change that—no discoveries, no inventions, no private griefs or sorrows or cares. Be fair when you meet any doubt about the Christian revelation; do not make light of any serious argument; but then never forget that your doubt has probably been met and answered a thousand times before you. Do not stand outside your faith with your doubt, but inside, where all the push and pressure of ages of trust and consolation can sweep the barrier away. Go on praying and worshiping and feeding on Him, and doubt not He will make it clear in the end.

When I see a man who has lived his life and met his trials, who has had his fears and his doubts, has toiled and ached, has lost and won, has stumbled and gone on, and through it all has kept his heart fixed on Christ, then it seems as though nothing in all the world was so glorious. He may never have satisfied his fears or answered his doubts, he may never have got any clear light on his problems, but through it all his heart rang true; there was never a syllable of uncertainty, never a moment when the deep needs of his heart did not call to the deep compassion of Christ, and he stood fast. Be one of those men; better be that than any prince or ruler or scholar or governor—a man of a fixed heart. How Christ will honor you! How He will look at you! There will come a moment to you and to me when the clouds will part and the darkness divide, when the heavens will open and the earth will fade, and the angels of God will be seen ascending and descending, and all things will be revealed. But more than that joy of finding out at last things hidden from the creation of the world will be the joy of standing face to face at last with the Lord on whom, through all the toil and the pain and the doubt of this world, the heart was fixed.

THE HOLY COMMUNION

St. John vi. 52.

The Jews therefore strove among themselves, saying, How can this man give us His flesh to eat?

THE HOLY COMMUNION

IT was the day before that our Lord miraculously fed the multitude which followed Him across the lake. You remember how the men were made to sit down, in number about five thousand, and how Jesus took the loaves, and blessed, and brake, and gave to all as much as they would. Then, seeing that the excited people wished to come and take Him by force and make Him a king, He departed again into a mountain alone; but on the next day our Lord spoke and plainly addressed Himself to all. " Ye seek Me," He said, . . . " because ye did eat of the loaves, and were filled. Labor not for the meat that perisheth, but for that meat that endureth unto everlasting life. . . . I am the living bread that cometh down from heaven: if any man eat of that bread, he shall live forever: and the bread that I will give is My flesh, which I will give for the life of the world. The Jews therefore strove among themselves, saying, How can this man give us His flesh to eat?"

That was a wonderful day in human history when our Lord declared the secret of all human strength; that was the sacramental moment of human history when our Lord opened the eyes of men and through a sign showed them the deep mysteries of life. Then all the past seemed plain, and all the future seemed transparent. There have always been turning-points in the life of man on the earth, when men saw the stream of destiny wheel visibly over into a new and providential course. There was a strange, distant day in the evolution of man when he discovered the use of iron and iron implements, and then the stone age, coarse and hard and brutal, came to an end. There was a wonderful day when the use of fire was first discovered, and savage men ceased to huddle in caves. There was the day of the invention of the compass, when the sea lost its terrors. There was the day of gunpowder, when the peasant found his freedom. There was the day of the printing-press, when free speech was born. There was the day of Immanuel Kant, the man who worked out the problem of all human thinking, and gave the signal of the French Revolution, and struck the key-note of an era of democracy. These were all passionate moments of freedom. But in the story of the human soul that on which all turns was the day when our Lord by a sacramental sign gave us His flesh to eat. Then through the outward sign of bread He showed His disciples how the heart of man is always and forever refreshed and sustained by feeding on the heart and mind of Christ, his Lord.

The Jews said with great astonishment, when they heard our Lord's words, "How can this man give us His flesh to eat?" It seems to many to-day a strange and incongruous interruption of the church's service. The world says with astonishment to-day, "How can this man give us His flesh to eat?"

Brethren, do we understand it ourselves? Do we know what we are about in the celebration of the holy communion? Do we understand why this sacrament stands there at the very center of the church's life and worship? Yes, there it is, the very center and pivot on which all turns. These vain and feeble words of mine are not the center of the church's worship; your wandering and imperfect prayers are not the center; our scanty offerings and efforts of work are not the center. No, but there it is, the blessed body and blood of Christ, on which all feed and from which all rise refreshed; that is the center and the soul of all.

Now the religion of Jesus Christ is mysterious, because it deals with the most mysterious thing in all the world, that is, human personality; but then the religion of Jesus Christ is the most intelligible thing in all the world, because we know more about personality than we know of anything else. We are ourselves persons, and one person can understand and absorb another person. The religion of Christ is hard to grasp, because it is so profound; but it is also easy to grasp, because it is so absolutely human. Christianity deals so squarely and entirely with the one thing in all the world that each man knows best, his own soul. Christianity is more thoughtful always than any other religion, because its sounding-line goes to depths that no other religion can reach; but Christianity is always less pedantic than any other religion; so much less pedantic than Buddhism, for example, with which it is often pedantically compared, because it speaks to every man in his mother speech. Much about Christianity there is which not the wisest man can fathom, but all that is needed to be brave and faithful and steadfast is within the reach of a trusting child. But the real way to get the proof of any truth of Christianity is to see its effect on human life. When you see Christian truth at work, then it seems to carry along with it its own conviction. Now the whole matter of this sacrament may be told in a word, that a man's heart always feeds on another's heart. Do you not know how true that is? The strength of one man's life always flows out to another and becomes food to that other. A man's courage, a man's insight, a man's experience, a man's patience, a man's form of character, these things flow out to weaker souls as surely as water flows down from a height above. A man's virtue is the one thing he cannot keep to himself. Every act of real nobleness becomes food to all those who witness it. Nobleness cannot be done, truth cannot be spoken, courage cannot be shown, without its making a difference to all other men. If you have done anything that is brave and true, you cannot prevent other souls from being fed by it. So the child feeds on all the character and the experience of the father; so the scholar feeds on all the wisdom of the teacher; so the soldier feeds on all the courage of his captain; so the painter feeds on all his master's skill. There is the mechanic who feeds on the power of the inventor; there is labor feeding on the guidance of the capital that employs it and makes it effective. The mind of one man is appropriated in a thousand workshops; the truth of one investigator is accepted by a thousand scholars; the songs of one poet are sung by a thousand lips; the holiness of one saint is strength to a thousand faltering men; and the body and blood of one Christ are the meat and the drink for all mankind.

You know men who by their mere presence

make you strong; you know men who exhilarate you and make you feel able to begin the struggle again. There is something far better than mere talent, and that is the power of a man to make his talent trusted. The wonderful thing about any human life is all the trust that it inspires. It is not the greatest thing to have talent; the greatest thing is to consecrate the talent you have. Any believing man makes all other men believers for the time being; any courageous man makes all other men courageous; any magnanimous man makes all other men magnanimous. There are men in whose presence one cannot be hard, cold, critical, unkind; they make one feel ashamed. The personal weight of Washington was felt through the whole army; the rectitude of Lincoln touched every man in the land. Character is really the most communicable thing in all the world; it cannot be confined; it exercises a subtle magnetism and inspires men. We are all the time absorbing the life of another; the lives of others are infused into our own. If there is any one whom you love and revere and look up to, you are feeding on the life of such a one. You know whether your life is food to any one else. Whoever is exerting any influence over you is giving you his flesh to eat. You are becoming changed through absorbing the personality of some one whom you admire; you are being unconsciously molded by another; you are seizing the ideas of another; you are accepting the standards and embracing the enthusiasms of another. Your mind gets its strength just as your body gets its strength—from what it feeds on. If there is no one whom you love, none whom you admire and revere, then your soul will be starved as truly as the body to which you denied its meat. What you honor, what you aim at, what you govern your life by, what you regard as right and what you regard as wrong, what you press toward and what you avoid, all that makes up your character. Where did you get it from? From those on whose character you have fed, from all whom you love and worship. Oh, has it not come chiefly from your blessed Lord?

The church tells you that there at the altar when you kneel is our Lord. Not in a figure merely, not in the mind merely, but really and truly present, there is Christ. There, at that sign of the broken bread and the poured-out wine, the earth quakes and the mortal veil is rent asunder, and we are with the Lord. Nothing is changed, and yet everything is changed, while the incarnate Son of God is before us. Everything that was before material becomes sacramental; everything that was before common and human becomes sacred and divine. Here is the human heart, and there is Christ; there is the Lamb that taketh away the sins of the world. Here are human sin and human burdens and human doubts and human sorrows, and there is divine succor and divine strength. Here is the famished heart of a man, and there is the bread that cometh down from heaven. Here is a man bent with this world's burdens, distracted with this world's craft, ashamed of this world's sinful pride, afflicted with this world's sorrows, and there is Christ saying the most absolutely human and yet divine word that ever lips have uttered: "This is My body, which is given for you: take and eat this in remembrance of Me."

The church's service seems almost to burst into a flame of glory in this sacrament; it is so divine and yet so human. Our church stands so strong here and is so much richer because she holds firmly both sides of the truth. She is Catholic, for she believes that Christ is really and truly present at the altar, and yet she is Protestant too, for she is consumed with the desire to be real and human and really and truly to build up men's souls by feeding them with Christ. Not the ascendancy of her priests, but the feeding the souls of weak and sinful men and women, is the church's one passionate aim. The sublime truth about the Incarnation is that God came *into* man's life. God and man became one blessed union.

Neither God nor man in Christ can be spared. So the sublime truth about the sacrament of the Lord's Supper is that Christ accepts these earthly elements as the signs of His real though spiritual presence. They remain unchanged as signs, though they speak of eternal things.

"How can this man give us His flesh to eat?" How can Christ help giving us His flesh to eat? How can our Lord keep us from adoring Him, from feeding on every word of pity that He spoke, and on every act of love and leadership? It was no dark and obscure commandment which our Lord laid on us when He said, "Do this in remembrance of Me." It was no strange duty hard to fulfil for all ages to come. Why, if Jesus had never said a word about the Lord's Supper, we should have gathered there just the same; we cannot help doing so. It belongs to the inextinguishable craving of a man's heart to feed on Christ; it belongs to a man's hunger and thirst after righteousness to feast on goodness wherever he sees it; and where should he find such goodness as with Christ? It springs out of our own weakness and helplessness and simpleness that we should have just this particular form of communion with the Lord. It was as inevitable that we should find in our faith the means of truly though spiritually feeding on the body and blood of Christ as that we should have a creed by which to confess His name, or prayers by which we should plead for His almighty deliverance.

Some of us are getting worn by the world. Some of us are losing heart, and our hopes are getting chilled. Some of us are lowering gradually the whole aim of our life, and are becoming half ready to stop fighting the old temptations, the old sins and infirmities, and are saying to ourselves incredulously, " How can this man give us His flesh to eat?" Brethren, you and I simply cannot help feeding on Christ. It is always life that quickens life, and character always fires character, and souls are fed always by the sacrifice of another soul. Take a fresh hold on Christ to-day; feed on Him to-day. You who are struggling with doubt and blinded in the storm of conflicting thoughts and feelings, come and kneel down and get your Lord's guidance. You who carry a great silent sorrow in your heart, do you want to keep from feeding on Him who raised up from the dead the widow's only son, and delivered him to his mother? You who have been bruised against the hardness of this world, can you help feeding on your Lord's compassion? You who have wept and have toiled, like the disciples, all the night, and have taken nothing, can you keep away from your Lord's table? You who are struggling against some long-standing sin, can you go on and live and work without your Lord's forgiveness and strength? Oh, how swiftly from the ends of the world Christ sweeps to the rescue of the heart that cries to Him, and says out of His infinite pity, "I am the living bread which came down from heaven: . . . and the bread that I will give is My flesh, which I will give for the life of the world."

3

www.ingramcontent.com/pod-product-compliance
Lightning Source LLC
Chambersburg PA
CBHW021814230426
43669CB00008B/747